Sixth Workshop on Cognitive Modeling and Computational Linguistics

(CMCL 2015)

Held at NAACL HLT 2015

Denver, Colorado, USA
4 June 2015

ISBN: 978-1-5108-0437-1

Printed from e-media with permission by:

Curran Associates, Inc.
57 Morehouse Lane
Red Hook, NY 12571

Some format issues inherent in the e-media version may also appear in this print version.

Printed by Curran Associates, Inc. (2015)

For permission requests, please contact the Association for Computational Linguistics at the address below.

Association for Computational Linguistics
209 N. Eighth Street
Stroudsburg, Pennsylvania 18360

Phone: 1-570-476-8006
Fax: 1-570-476-0860

acl@aclweb.org

Additional copies of this publication are available from:

Curran Associates, Inc.
57 Morehouse Lane
Red Hook, NY 12571 USA
Phone: 845-758-0400
Fax: 845-758-2634
Email: curran@proceedings.com
Web: www.proceedings.com

Introduction

The papers in these proceedings were presented at the 6th annual workshop on Cognitive Modeling and Computational Linguistics (CMCL), held in Denver, Colorado on June 4th, 2015. As with earlier CMCL meetings, CMCL 2015 provided a venue to support a broad spectrum of computational psycholinguistic inquiry. This year, we were pleased to receive fifteen submissions, ten of which were selected for final presentation at the workshop and are included in these proceedings. The submissions this year were exceptionally strong and reviewers commented that many of them could easily have been accepted as main conference submissions. We would like to thank all submitting authors for the quality and variety of the papers we received, and we would like to thank the program committee for their time, expertise, and insightful comments on the submissions. Thanks to the generous support of our sponsors, The Center for Cognitive and Brain Sciences at The Ohio State University and The Ohio State University Department of Linguistics, we were able to obtain invited speakers and provide travel grants to a number of student authors. We extend our appreciation to our invited speakers, Dr. Andrew Kehler of the University of California, San Diego and Dr. Mark Steedman of the University of Edinburgh, for sharing their work with us. Thanks to everyone for your continued support of this workshop and for helping to foster the growth of the field of computational psycholinguistics.

Marten van Schijndel and Tim O'Donnell

Organizers:

Tim O'Donnell, MIT

Marten van Schijndel, The Ohio State University

Program Committee:

Omri Abend, University of Edinburgh

Steven Abney, University of Michigan

Afra Alishahi, Tilburg University

Libby Barak, University of Toronto

Marco Baroni, University of Trento

Robert Berwick, MIT

Klinton Bicknell, Northwestern University

Christos Christodoulopoulos, University of Illinois at Urbana-Champaign

Alexander Clark, King's College

Moreno Coco, University of Lisbon

Jennifer Culbertson, George Mason University

Vera Demberg, Saarland University

Brian Dillon, University of Massachusetts Amherst

Micha Elsner, The Ohio State University

Naomi Feldman, University of Maryland

Alex Fine, University of Illinois at Urbana-Champaign

Bob Frank, Yale University

Michael Frank, Stanford University

Stefan Frank, Radboud University Nijmegen

Stella Frank, Edinburgh University

Ted Gibson, MIT

Sharon Goldwater, Edinburgh University

Carlos Gomez Gallo, Northwestern University

Noah Goodman, Stanford University

Thomas Graf, Stony Brook University

John Hale, Cornell University

Jeffrey Heinz, University of Delaware

Tim Hunter, University of Minnesota
Mark Johnson, Macquarie University
Frank Keller, University of Edinburgh
Shalom Lappin, King's College
Roger Levy, UCSD
Pavel Logacev, Potsdam University
Titus von der Malsburg, UCSD
Rebecca Morley, The Ohio State University
Aida Nematzadeh, University of Toronto
Ulrike Pado, Hochschule fuer Technik, Stuttgart
Bozena Pajak, Northwestern University
Lisa Pearl, UC Irvine
Massimo Poesio, University of Essex
Ting Qian, Brown University
Roi Reichart, Technion University
David Reitter, Penn State University
William Schuler, The Ohio State University
Nathaniel Smith, University of Edinburgh
Ed Stabler, UCLA
Mark Steedman, University of Edinburgh
Patrick Sturt, University of Edinburgh
Colin Wilson, Johns Hopkins University
Alessandra Zarcone, Saarland University
Jelle Zuidema, University of Amsterdam

Invited Speakers:

Andrew Kehler, University of California, San Diego
Mark Steedman, University of Edinburgh

Table of Contents

Conference Program

Thursday, June 4, 2015

08:55–09:00 Opening Remarks

09:00–10:00 Invited Talk by Andrew Kehler

10:00–10:30 *Predictions for self-priming from incremental updating models unifying comprehension and production*
Cassandra L. Jacobs

10:30–11:00 Coffee Break

11:00–11:30 *Pragmatic Alignment on Social Support Type in Health Forum Conversations*
Yafei Wang, John Yen and David Reitter

11:30–12:00 *Audience size and contextual effects on information density in Twitter conversations*
Gabriel Doyle and Michael Frank

12:00–12:30 *Centre Stage: How Social Network Position Shapes Linguistic Coordination*
Bill Noble and Raquel Fernandez

12:30–13:30 Lunch Break

13:30–14:00 *Fusion of Compositional Network-based and Lexical Function Distributional Semantic Models*
Spiros Georgiladakis, Elias Iosif and Alexandros Potamianos

14:00–14:30 *Verb polysemy and frequency effects in thematic fit modeling*
Clayton Greenberg, Vera Demberg and Asad Sayeed

14:30–15:00 *An Evaluation and Comparison of Linguistic Alignment Measures*
Yang Xu and David Reitter

15:00–15:30 *Utility-based evaluation metrics for models of language acquisition: A look at speech segmentation*
Lawrence Phillips and Lisa Pearl

15:30–16:00 Coffee Break

Thursday, June 4, 2015 (continued)

16:00–16:30 *Evidence of syntactic working memory usage in MEG data*
Marten van Schijndel, Brian Murphy and William Schuler

16:30–17:00 *Modeling fMRI time courses with linguistic structure at various grain sizes*
John Hale, David Lutz, Wen-Ming Luh and Jonathan Brennan

17:00–18:00 Invited Talk by Mark Steedman

Predictions for self-priming from incremental updating models unifying comprehension and production

Cassandra L. Jacobs
Department of Psychology
University of Illinois at Urbana-Champaign
603 E. Daniel St.
Champaign, IL 61820
cljacob2@illinois.edu

Abstract

Syntactic priming from comprehension to production has been shown to be robust: we are more likely to repeat structures that we have previously heard. Many current models do not distinguish between comprehension and production. Here we contrast human language processing with two variants of a Bayesian belief updating model. In the first model, production-to-production priming (i.e. self-priming) is as strong as comprehension-to-production priming. In the second, both individuals who self-prime and those who do not are exposed to a syntactic construction via comprehension. Our results suggest that when production-to-production priming is as robust as comprehension-to-production priming, then speakers who self-prime are simultaneously less likely to be primed by input from comprehension and demonstrate different distributions of responses than speakers who do not self-prime. The computational model accords with recent results demonstrating no self-priming, and provides evidence for an account of syntactic priming that distinguishes between production and comprehension input.

1 Introduction

Syntactic priming in production is the increased probability of using a syntactic structure when we have recently encountered it. Many models of syntactic priming treat comprehension and production as equally influential on the language production system (Pickering & Garrod, 2013; Chang et al., 2006; Reitter et al., 2011). This means that syntactic priming can occur without another person being present, from production to production (self-priming). Unfortunately, little experimental research has assessed the degree to which priming occurs from production to production in a controlled context.

The primary phenomena that are of interest to research on syntactic priming are as follows: (1) Do we incrementally and cumulatively adapt to our linguistic environment, changing how we talk based on what we hear (Jaeger & Snider, 2013; Chang et al., 2006; Kaschak et al., 2012; Reitter et al., 2011; Pickering & Garrod, 2013)? (2) Do we change how we talk more when we encounter less probable structures (Jaeger & Snider, 2013; Chang et al., 2006)? (3) How long-lasting is syntactic priming (Kaschak, 2007; Bock, 1986)? And finally: (4) Are we more likely to repeat the structures that we ourselves have said, as predicted by models that unify priming in comprehension and production (Pickering & Garrod, 2013; Chang et al., 2006)? The model presented here accounts for these phenomena and makes additional predictions about the potential ramifications of self-priming on linguistic representations and efficient communication.

2 Psycholinguistic evidence

In any model where speakers are influenced by their prior experience, regardless of the source, priming should occur. Corpus linguistics has provided evidence of self-priming in production. Some of these studies assessed priming of specific constructions such as the dative alternation or relative clauses

Proceedings of CMCL 2015, pages 1–8,
Denver, Colorado, June 4, 2015. ©2015 Association for Computational Linguistics

(Jaeger & Snider, 2013; Myslin & Levy, submitted) or instead model the whole syntactic system using probabilistic rules in several grammatical formalisms (Gries, 2005; Healey et al., 2014; Reitter et al., 2011). These models generally find evidence for syntactic priming from production to production, or structural repetition that occurs more often than would be expected by chance. In contrast to some of these results, some studies report that structural repetition occurs less than would be expected by chance (Healey et al., 2014). Healey et al. (2014) argued that this is because speakers avoid continuously reusing syntactic structures.

The evidence for self-priming in a more controlled environment is weaker. Within experimental psycholinguistics, structural priming in production is almost always mediated by some intervening comprehension task like sentence completion or a memory task (e.g. Kaschak, 2007, Bock, 1986, etc.), making it difficult or impossible to assess whether self-priming occurs. Some studies have reported that some speakers have an almost uniform bias toward one structure or another (e.g. Jaeger & Snider, 2013). However, despite these claims that comprehension and production show similar amounts of syntactic priming (Tooley & Bock, 2014), production has also been shown to be substantially less flexible than comprehension (Remez, 2013). Syntactic persistence within a speaker could simply be a product of an individual's own syntactic preferences rather than self-priming per se.

Some experimental work has been conducted to test whether comprehension and production are weighted equally in structural priming in production. Counter to what has been found in corpus studies, Jacobs et al. (2015) failed to find evidence for self-priming despite strong comprehension-to-production priming. In their study, participants produced 7 dative descriptions, comprehended 6 dative descriptions of a single form of the construction, and produced an additional 7 descriptions in order to identify effects of self-priming, individual differences, and comprehension input on the magnitude of comprehension-to-production priming. They found that the rates of structural repetition were flat across the experiment, but speakers were strongly sensitive to comprehension input, showing large and sustained comprehension-to-production priming effects. They also found larger priming effects for the less probable syntactic structure, consistent with error-driven learning accounts of the inverse frequency effect (Jaeger & Snider, 2013).

While the evidence for self-priming has been weaker, almost all syntactic priming studies have demonstrated that comprehension plays a very large role in production preferences. This is to be expected if priming is a means of achieving efficient communication, which requires using comprehended language to modify our own productions to be more easily understood (Pickering & Garrod, 2013; Tooley & Bock, 2014). It is less clear what the functional role of self-priming would be, however. If speakers are likely to repeat structures they have recently used, the language community may end up with two types of speakers: those who only use one structure or the other, which would pose some difficulty for comprehenders (MacDonald, 2013).

We aim to address the question of the equivalence of learning from comprehension and production, as well as account for the results of Jacobs et al. (2015). To do this, we constructed a very simple Bayesian belief-updating model that makes predictions about syntactic preferences with and without self-priming. This model is very similar to those of Fine et al. (2010), Kleinschmidt et al. (2012), and Myslin & Levy (submitted), who have modeled updating in syntactic comprehension. These models perform Bayesian belief-updating of the probabilities of outcomes in a syntactic alternation. In ours, we focus on the prepositional versus double object dative, though the model can be extended to any syntactic alternation. In the computational model, we demonstrate differences at the individual and population levels differences between self-priming and no self-priming (Model 1), as well as characterize what self-priming does to syntactic adaptation in production after comprehension (Model 2).

3 Model structure

Many of the recent computational models that have sought to account for syntactic priming effects in comprehension and production use incremental algorithms to represent trial-by-trial effects, while also treating experience in comprehension and production as contributing equally to the implicit learning process (Jaeger & Snider, 2013; Chang et al., 2006; Reitter et al., 2011; Pickering & Garrod, 2013). The model here is simple but relies on similar assumptions: representations are changed when language is processed.

Each utterance choice can be conceptualized as a single coin flipped randomly (i.e. a binomial process). We generate sequences of utterances by sampling from either a static Binomial distribution or one that is continually being updated. The structural alternation we consider here is the double object dative construction, which has been extensively studied in syntactic priming experiments (Jaeger & Snider, 2013; Kaschak, 2007; Bock, 1986; Pickering & Garrod, 2013). In this syntactic alternation, direct and indirect objects can change places after some English verbs like *give*, *hand*, *throw*, or *show*:

- The librarian gave the book to the boy. (prepositional object - PO)

- The librarian gave the boy the book. (double object - DO)

For every sentence a speaker intends to use a dative structure, the production system will select either the PO or the DO form of the sentence. Selections are single samples from a Binomial distribution with *p*(PO) = .55, which was derived from the empirical probability of individuals producing a PO in Jacobs et al. (2015).

Previous models have used error-driven learning to account for incremental adjustments in syntactic preferences (Jaeger & Snider, 2013; Chang et al., 2006). In our model, as in similar models, we update the probability of using a PO using the Beta prior, which is conjugate to the Binomial distribution. This prior is also appropriate because in any syntactic alternation, there are two possible outcomes. The Beta distribution has only two hyperparameters, α and β. α roughly corresponds to the number of times the model believes that it has experienced a PO dative, and β represents the analogous number for the DO dative.

The selection of the α and β values was based on exploring an integer-valued parameter space between 1 and 10 for both parameters. In Figure 1 we plot the amount of self-priming all 100 models demonstrated as a function of the two hyperparameters. We determined that α does not influence the sensitivity the model has to its own productions. Contrarily, β values on the smaller end tended to lead to large self-priming effects. Consequently we chose identical values for α and β that would allow for both self-priming and sensitivity to comprehension input. This was therefore a compromise between flexibility and rigidity.

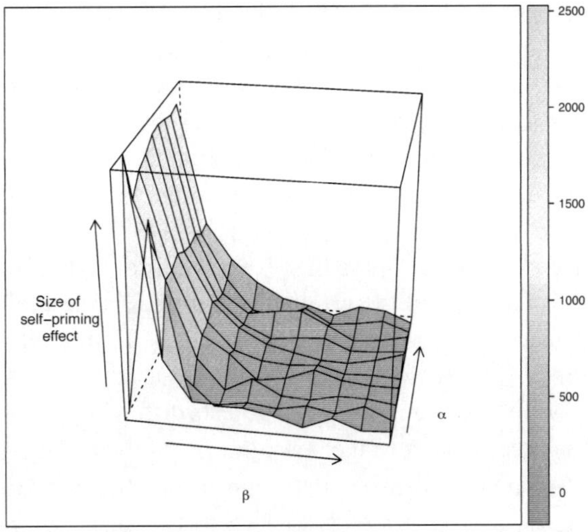

Figure 1: As values of α and β increase from 1 to 10, the models become less capable of self-priming. At the smallest values of β, the model is very sensitive to its own prior productions, while α does not seem to play a large role in self-priming.

We initialized the model with relatively weak, but not completely unbiased, priors that both structures were equally possible: $\alpha = 4$, $\beta = 4$. We assume that one of the structures is slightly more probable, with *p*(PO) = .55, as observed in Jacobs et al. (2015).

With every subsequent dative description that the model processes (either via production or comprehension), with *k* POs and *n* descriptions containing either a DO or a PO, the priors are adjusted via the following update rules:

$$\alpha = \alpha + k \tag{1}$$

$$\beta = \beta + n - k \tag{2}$$

The new probability of a PO is therefore:

$$p(PO) = \frac{\alpha + k + 1}{\alpha + \beta + n - 2} \tag{3}$$

For both Model 1 and Model 2, we ran 1000 "experiments" of 200 "participants" each. Model 1 looks at the production of seven double object datives to assess self-priming. Model 2 is structured like the experiments of Jacobs et al. (2015) and consists of three stages. First, seven datives are produced, then six datives of a single syntactic structure are comprehended, and then seven additional datives are produced. In the production tasks, participants' syntactic choices were randomly sampled from a Binomial distribution initialized at $p(\text{PO}) = .55$. This allows us to treat individual subjects differently prior to exposing them to the comprehension materials.

The model always updates the probability of a PO when it encounters a PO or DO. In Model 1 we assess what should happen to participants' later productions if they are influenced by their own productions (self-prime) to the same extent as in comprehension. In Model 2 we look at the magnitude of comprehension-to-production priming when participants are allowed to self-prime versus not.

4 Model 1 - Self-priming in production

This task can be conceptualized as a spontaneous production task. We conducted 1000 experiments with 200 participants each. Each participant produces seven sentences. Participants' syntactic choices are sampled from an incrementally updating Binomial distribution where the calculated posterior probability for each subject replaces the prior probability of $p(\text{PO})$. Each utterance that the model produces contains either a prepositional object dative construction (e.g. *The librarian gave the book to the boy*) or a double object dative (e.g. *The librarian gave the boy the book*).

Qualitatively, the model makes the prediction that, in general, models where self-priming occurs should be more likely to prefer one form of a structure over the other. Self-priming increases the entropy of the distribution, though it is naturally biased toward producing more probable structures since those are initially more likely to be drawn. We summarize the results of our simulations for self-primers and non self-primers below in Figure 2.

Importantly, self-priming always produces some change to the model parameters. At the limit, the production system's predictions are often correct, leading to minimal prediction error (e.g. Chang, Dell, & Bock, 2006; Jaeger & Snider, 2013). A lack of prediction error can be conceptualized as the same thing as no self-priming in production, since neither leads to changes in syntactic preferences. Analogously, as the hyperparameters increase for an individual iteration of the model, the more confident the model is in its initial representations, leading to a stable distribution for a single speaker. It is also possible, however, that production and comprehension are updated separately, but production possesses more conservative hyperparameters, in line with research showing the static preferences of the production system (Remez, 2013).

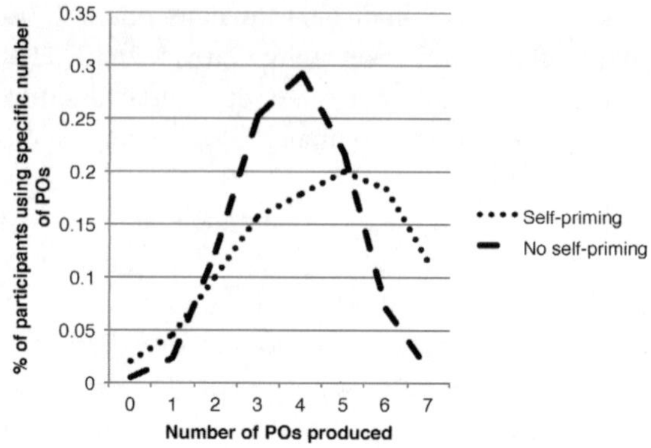

Figure 2: Self-priming without adjustment from comprehension results in a more uniform distribution of syntactic preferences across a population of speakers than in a model where speakers do not prime themselves.

The bulk of priming occurs early in the experiment. Participants' prior productions should play an influential role on their later productions, with the population's structural preferences stabilizing over the course of seven trials. This implies that prediction error made by the model decreases over many productions by a single speaker. We visualize this below in Figure 3.

5 Model 2 - Transfer from comprehension to production

We wanted to see how much self-priming diminishes the effect of comprehension-to-production priming, since self-priming changes the hyperparameters of the model, meaning that the model becomes more conservative in its estimates of the probability of us-

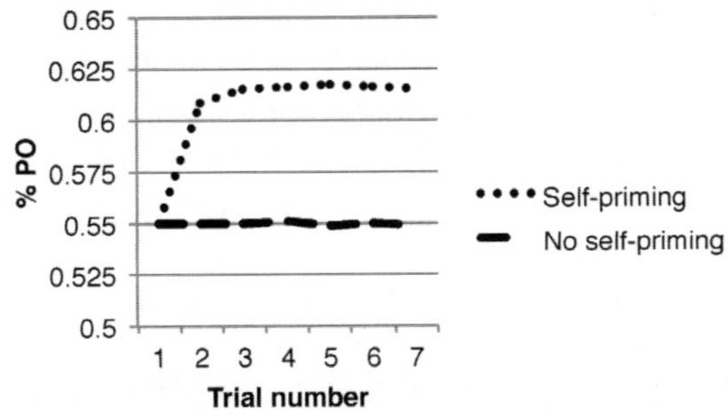

Figure 3: Models where self-priming is permitted converge on preferring the higher-probability structure within two trials. Models that do not permit self-priming show the same syntactic bias over the course of the experiment.

ing a PO (that is, the values of both α and β are larger). This experiment is structured in the same way as Model 1, except participants later comprehend 1 or 6 utterances containing a single structure (DOs or POs only) and produce an additional seven utterances in a final production task, following the experimental design of Jacobs et al. (2015).

Priming from comprehension to production is accomplished via the same updating process that we defined above. When a participant encounters a DO or PO structure, this updates the α and β parameters, and the observed posterior probability replaces the prior probability of a PO. The α and β parameters after comprehension are therefore adjusted in favor of the primed structure, which makes the primed structure more likely to be drawn on the next trial.

The model changes more for low-probability structures. Because the model has flexible priors, after hearing a single structure for six consecutive trials, the model will believe that the primed structure, regardless of which structure was primed, will be a certain likelihood (e.g. p(PO) or p(DO) = .75) after the comprehension stage. The model therefore shows more priming after exposure to the less common structure (DO) than after exposure to the more probable structure (PO). The model here demonstrates greater priming for dispreferred structures because the gap to bridge is larger for the dispreferred structure. Our results accord with models that employ error-based learning principles (Chang et al., 2006; Jaeger & Snider, 2013), where model parameters are adjusted via experience and change more in response to lower-probability structures. Figure 4 summarizes the relationship between prime probability, self-priming, and cumulativity.

Self-priming leads to much smaller effects of priming from comprehension. Even when exposed to a relatively high number of primes (6 versus 1), participants who self-prime do not align to comprehension input as much as participants who are not affected by their own prior productions. This is because the hyperparameters are tuned an additional seven trials before these participants go into the comprehension stage of the experiment, which makes it more difficult to change the probability distribution on later trials. Should the non self-priming models' hyperparameters be set sufficiently high, to perhaps the same level as the average self-priming model, this particular difference would likely disappear. Additionally, if hyperparameters for both models were even higher, it is likely that the magnitude of priming would not differ much between the two model types. Keeping the hyperparameters small before relevant linguistic experience (via comprehension or via both comprehension and production), makes it easier to see that self-primers require more comprehension input to offset their learned production biases.

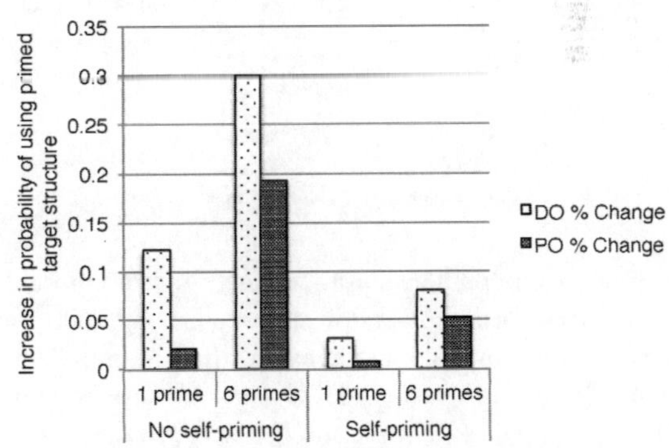

Figure 4: Increase in use of primed target structures in the second half of the experiment as a function of the number of primes, whether the models self-prime or not, and which structure was primed. All models accommodate the comprehension input. Priming is strongest when the primed structure was less frequent (DO). Similarly, when participants are exposed to more primes (6 versus 1), the priming effects are larger. Self-primers show smaller priming effects in all cases.

To assess the possibility that having high values of α and β diminishes the effect of comprehension-to-production priming, we ran an additional set of experiments with α and β set to 40 and 50, respectively. These values were selected to produce a probability of p(PO) roughly equal to .55. This experiment definitively demonstrated that an additional 6 primes of a particular structure still results in change to the model, though the non self-priming model is much more sensitive to six items of a single structure than the self-priming model, which has stronger beliefs about p(PO). The self-priming model seems inclined to not accommodate at all (.4% change), while the non self-priming model changes at a measurable amount (3%, comparable to the self-priming model that received 1 prime in Figure 4). The results of these simulations are demonstrated below in Figure 5. This suggests that even when the model's hyperparameters are made to be very conservative, self-priming is detrimental to comprehension-to-production priming.

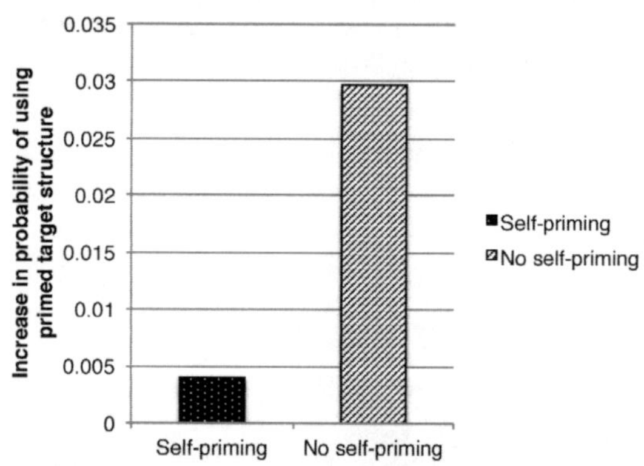

Figure 5: In comprehension-to-production priming models where self-priming is allowed to occur, the ability to accommodate novel comprehension input is greatly reduced. The self-priming model changes toward the comprehension input .4%, while the non self-priming model changes 3%.

6 Comparison to psycholinguistic data

An important test of the model is to compare its output to existing psycholinguistic data. While the model can account neither for the corpus linguistic studies that have demonstrated repetition greater than would be expected by chance (Jaeger & Snider, 2013; Reitter et al., 2011; Gries, 2005; Myslin & Levy, submitted), nor for those studies reporting speakers with strong structural biases (Jaeger & Snider, 2013), nor for anti-repetition and decay (Healey et al., 2014; Reitter et al., 2011), it can account for several phenomena that have been well-demonstrated in structural priming in production, as well as the results of Jacobs et al. (2015).

Self-priming is predicted by many accounts of syntactic priming where comprehension and production input are equated (Chang et al., 2006; Pickering & Garrod, 2013; Jaeger & Snider, 2013; Tooley & Bock, 2014). We have demonstrated here that self-priming leads to self-convergence. In a model where one's own prior productions weigh in on one's later productions, speakers quickly converge on a syntactic preference, with the majority of speakers coming to prefer the more probable structure (Figure 2). These results are counter to the experimental results of Jacobs et al. (2015), who reported that repetition of syntactic structures was constant at all stages of the production task. Had speakers primed themselves, the probability of using the more probable structure should have increased, however modestly (Figure 3).

Models allowing for self-priming with sufficiently large hyperparameters (Figure 1) would likely show both very little self-priming (having converged on a particular syntactic preference) as well as relatively little sensitivity to comprehension input (Figure 4). This is again counter to the results of Jacobs et al. (2015), who found very large comprehension-to-production structural priming effects. Production and comprehension sharing hyperparameters leads to radically different results than what is empirically observed.

Altogether, the computational model and the experimental data suggest that comprehension and production should be modeled separately. In order to obtain a production system that maintains its own internal representations *and* accommodates comprehension input (Remez, 2013; Pickering & Garrod, 2013), it is important that speakers not overweight their own syntactic preferences. This can be accomplished by having separate production and comprehension systems, where production-to-production priming (updating) is minimal while comprehension-to-production priming is large. An alternative, as described in Model 2, is to only allow updating from comprehension to production.

The model agrees with both existing computational models of syntactic priming and psycholinguistic data. The model updates incrementally, as many others have done (Chang et al., 2006; Jaeger & Snider, 2013; Fine et al., 2010; Kleinschmidt et al., 2012) and shows greater priming effects when exposed to multiple instances of the same structure (Kaschak et al., 2012). The priming effects are larger for less common structures than for more common structures because of the sensitivity of the model to error, demonstrating the inverse frequency effect (Chang et al., 2006; Jaeger & Snider, 2013). Finally, in a model where self-priming does not occur, or where updating from production to production is extremely low, structural preferences persist (Reitter et al., 2011; Tooley & Bock, 2014; Bock & Griffin, 2000; Kaschak, 2007; Kaschak et al., 2012).

7 Conclusion

The present model accounts for the incrementality, cumulativity, error sensitivity, and persistence of syntactic priming in production. In contrast to previous models of syntactic priming (Jaeger & Snider, 2013; Chang et al., 2006; Reitter et al., 2011; Pickering & Garrod, 2013), we tested the effects of equating comprehension and production input in structural priming in production. Self-priming has consequences for both individual and population-level language use.

This model makes predictions for all of these phenomena by making a single assumption: prior experience affects syntactic choices in production. Regardless of whether self-priming is allowed to occur or not, we are sensitive to recent and cumulative linguistic input and are primed to produce the structures we hear. Additionally, we change our representations more when we encounter low-probability structures. Because syntactic representations are updated without respect to time, syntactic priming effects do not necessarily decay in this model as in others (e.g. Reitter et al., 2011). However, most syntactic priming studies report structural persistence, making the model consistent with such studies (Bock, 1986; Tooley & Bock, 2014; Bock & Griffin, 2000; Kaschak et al., 2012). Finally, if individuals are allowed to self-prime, priming from comprehension will be weak and a population of speakers may be very variable in their structural preferences.

The functional value of self-priming is tempting if language is structured optimally to be easy for the speaker (MacDonald, 2013). Speakers can employ their own syntactic preferences, with comprehenders accommodating them. Other theories have stated that priming between speakers is necessary for efficient communication (Pickering & Garrod, 2013; Jaeger & Snider, 2013), especially because speakers must learn the distributions of the language around them in order to become successful communicators (Chang et al., 2006). In a language community, it may be sufficient to accommodate conversation partners rather than to develop highly idiosyncratic production preferences, making self-priming and structural repetition sub-optimal (Healey et al., 2014). At the same time, comprehenders are sensitive to the repetitive nature of conversations and may come to expect repetition during dialogue (Myslin & Levy, submitted). To that end, we are extending this model to simulate population dynamics in communities where speakers prime each other and possibly also prime themselves. Self-priming has consequences for language-level statistics, so it is important to see what changes might take place in a language community where individual speakers are allowed to become highly idiosyncratic.

It is still an open question as to whether one's own productions influence later syntactic choices. Some more recent psycholinguistic evidence suggests that they do not (Jacobs et al., 2015). If speakers do not self-prime, is it because they tend to avoid repeating syntactic structures (e.g. Healey et al., 2014), or is there an error-driven learning component, where predictions about one's own production are almost always correct, leading to no learning? To answer these questions, further experimental work is needed. In the meantime, we have outlined some predictions and accounted for the vast majority of phenomena in syntactic priming in production with a very simple belief-updating model.

References

Bock, J. K. (1986). Syntactic persistence in language production. *Cognitive Psychology, 18*, 355–387.

Bock, K., & Griffin, Z. M. (2000). The persistence of structural priming: Transient activation or implicit learning? *Journal of Experimental Psychology: General, 129*, 177–192.

Chang, F., Dell, G. S., & Bock, K. (2006). Becoming syntactic. *Psychological Review, 113*, 234–272.

Fine, A. B., Qian, T., Jaeger, T. F., & Jacobs, R. A. (2010). Syntactic adaptation in language comprehension. *Proceedings of ACL Workshop on Cognitive Modeling and Computational Linguistics*, (pp. 18–26).

Gries, S. T. (2005). Syntactic priming: A corpus-based approach. *Journal of Psycholinguistic Research, 34*, 365–399.

Healey, P. G. T., Purver, M., & Howes, C. (2014). Divergence in dialogue. *PLoS ONE, 9*, e98598.

Jacobs, C. L., Bock, K., & Watson, D. G. (2015). Speakers do not self-prime. *Poster presented at CUNY Conference on Sentence Processing, University of Southern California, Los Angeles.*.

Jaeger, T. F., & Snider, N. E. (2013). Alignment as a consequence of expectation adaptation: Syntactic priming is affected by the prime's prediction error given both prior and recent experience. *Cognition, 127*, 57–83.

Kaschak, M. P. (2007). Long-term structural priming affects subsequent patterns of language production. *Memory & Cognition, 35*, 925–937.

Kaschak, M. P., Kutta, T. J., & Coyle, J. M. (2012). Long and short term cumulative structural priming effects. *Language, Cognition and Neuroscience, 29*, 728–743.

Kleinschmidt, D., Fine, A. B., & Jaeger, T. F. (2012). A belief-updating model of adaptation and cue combination in syntactic comprehension. *Proceedings of the 34rd Annual Meeting of the Cognitive Science Society (CogSci12)*, (pp. 605–610).

MacDonald, M. C. (2013). How language production shapes language form and comprehension. *Frontiers in Psychology, 4*.

Myslin, M., & Levy, R. (submitted). Comprehension priming as rational expectation for repetition: Evidence from syntactic processing. *Cognition*.

Pickering, M. J., & Garrod, S. (2013). An integrated theory of language production and comprehension. *Behavioral and Brain Sciences, 36*, 329–347.

Reitter, D., Keller, F., & Moore, J. D. (2011). A computational cognitive model of syntactic priming. *Cognitive Science, 35*, 587–637.

Remez, R. E. (2013). Analogy and disanalogy in production and perception of speech. *Language, Cognition and Neuroscience, 30*, 273–286.

Tooley, K. M., & Bock, K. (2014). On the parity of structural persistence in language production and comprehension. *Cognition, 132*, 101–136.

Pragmatic Alignment on Social Support Type in Health Forum Conversations

Yafei Wang, John Yen, David Reitter
College of Information Sciences and Technology
The Pennsylvania State University
University Park, PA 16801, USA
yxw184@psu.edu, jyen@ist.psu.edu, reitter@psu.edu

Abstract

Linguistic alignment, such as lexical and syntactic alignment, is a universal phenomenon influencing dialogue participants in online conversations. While adaptation can occur at lexical, syntactic and pragmatic levels, relationships between alignments at multiple levels are neither theoretically nor empirically well understood. In this study, we find that community members show pragmatic alignment on social support type, distinguishing emotional and informational support, both of which provide benefits to members. We also find that lexical alignment is correlated with emotional support. This finding can contribute to our understanding of the linguistic signature of different types of support as well as the theory of Interactive Alignment in dialogue.

1 Introduction

Linguistic alignment is a psycholinguistic phenomenon that causes dialogue participants to adjust their language patterns to those of their conversation partners. These linguistic patterns include words (Gries, 2005), syntax (Bock, 1986; Branigan et al., 2000; Jaeger and Snider, 2007), gestures (Bergmann and Kopp, 2012) and more. This phenomenon has been well examined and explored under experimental settings (Fusaroli et al., 2012; Reitter and Moore, 2007), in naturalistic discourse (Gries, 2005; Reitter et al., 2006), as well as in online conversations (Huffaker et al., 2006; Scissors et al., 2008; Backstrom et al., 2013), social media, and fictional dialogue in film scripts (Danescu-Niculescu-Mizil and Lee, 2011). Moreover, according to the Interactive Alignment Model (IAM) (Pickering and Garrod, 2004), linguistic alignment has been suspected to be a driver of mutual understanding, building up over different levels (lexicon, syntax, situation, pragmatic, agreement).

Alignment is a universal phenomenon that reaches beyond the linguistic decisions we make once we have decided to communicate an idea. *Pragmatics* is commonly taken to refer to the way we express and understand communications in context, encoding higher-level intent. How people understand words and phrases in a given situation is indeed subject to alignment (Garrod and Anderson, 1987). Generally, games can elucidate pragmatic reasoning and mutual adaptation thereof (Frank and Goodman, 2012). To the best of our knowledge, there is no prior report of pragmatic alignment in naturalistic situations. For the purposes of this study, we define the pragmatics of an utterance as the intended effect on the reader or listener, regardless of the way it is semantically expressed. Unlike in pragmatics in linguistics, however, our focus is not on the differences between explicitly stated and implied meaning.

The first question this paper will focus on is analyzing pragmatic alignment in naturalistic dialogue, specifically in internet forum conversation. To understand what we mean by higher-level semantics or pragmatics in these data, we need to understand the motivation and dynamics of these communities.

An increasing number of people with serious

Proceedings of CMCL 2015, pages 9–18,

disease seek and give social support in group discussions in online social networks such as Facebook and online health support communities. Basically, there are four types of social support, emotional support, informational support, tangible/instrumental support and appraisal support (Langford et al., 1997; Malecki and Demaray, 2003). In online communities, the social support exchange is primarily of an informational or emotional nature (Wang et al., 2012; Rimer et al., 2005). Understandably, people with a life-threatening illness are in need of both information, such as side-effects of a specific drug, and emotional care, such as empathy. Previous research on behavior analysis, such as stress-buffering theory (Cohen and McKay, 1984), also suggested that exchanging useful social support protects people from stressful and pathological events. Analyzing the social support and the kind of support conveyed in the messages will be of benefit to support-oriented community building. Furthermore, previous studies (Zhao et al., 2014) suggested that earlier responses to a new support seeking request help predict leaders in self-supported communities. Although, the proportion of emotional or informational support in a message can, of course, be influenced by many factors, such as previous messages in the conversation, word choices and personality. Nevertheless, we use this measure for further analysis. From the alignment perspective, we will focus on whether people tend to align in the type of support in online health communities. In other words, we first analyze the pragmatic alignment phenomenon, which is defined as alignment of the type of support provided by one community member to another. We validate it in one of the largest online health communities, Cancer Survivor Network. To the best of our knowledge, pragmatic alignment in online communities has not been explored yet.

The second question is whether we could find evidence for or against the Interactive Alignment Model (Pickering and Garrod, 2004) in this dataset. As IAM suggested, alignment at different levels is linked, building up from lower-level adaptation. At a functional level, linguistic alignment indicates and may help build social relationships (Danescu-Niculescu-Mizil and Lee, 2011), reveal social status (Danescu-Niculescu-Mizil et al., 2011; Jones et al., 2014) and strengthen situational awareness in dialogic tasks (Fusaroli et al., 2012; Reitter and Moore, 2007, 2014).

Thus, an important question in this context is whether adaptation also applies to higher-level pragmatic goals, such as providing support that is more informational or more emotional. Convergence at lower levels would theoretically be expected to correlate to higher-level convergence, and conversations that show convergence would be expected to be more effective. Do priming effects at levels of lexicon and syntax influence the proportion of the type of support in a message within the conversation? We predict that social support adaptation exists in thread based discussions. Theoretically, we would also expect that low-level priming facilitates any social support adaptation we find.

To sum up, there are two concrete questions we will address in this paper:

- **(1)** Does the type of support (i.e, emotional vs. informational) provided by early responders (i.e, first responder) on a thread influence the type of support provided by later responders in self-support communities?
- **(2)** Does lexical and syntactic alignment (henceforth "linguistic alignment") between early responders and later responders correlate to the type of support matching?

The alignment we are concerned with would clearly happen at the level of communicative intent. We consider this *pragmatics*. The pragmatics we refer to is not the same as it's used in linguistics concerning contextual and indirect interpretation of sentence semantics, but rather the sense of intent, in a psychological sense. In psychology, pragmatic communication comprises social and conventional messages that take the recipient's needs into account. Social support adaptation specifically considers the unspoken rule that we perceive an interlocutor's emotional and informational needs and react accordingly.

Some studies in behavior analysis (Backstrom et al., 2013; Cheng et al., 2014) showed that word use in the conversations may influence members' behavior in the communities. Althoff et al. (2014) stated that request presentation influences members' feedbacks in a variety of ways, such as sentiment, politeness and length of reply posts. Cheng et al. (2014) mentioned that members' feedbacks also shapes users' behavior in the communities. Furthermore, automated content (Qiu et al., 2011) and discourse analysis using machine learning methods provided important insights about the benefits and causal relationships (Bui et al., 2015) with support behaviors in online health communities. Thus, modeling members' feedbacks at the pragmatic level could help us build better communities.

A recent study from Vlahovic et al. (2014) was similar to our study. They used profit regression to predict members' satisfaction after receiving emotional and informational support in a breast cancer online support community. For one thread, a trained profit regression model predicted the thread initiators' satisfaction scale from 1 to 7. In this study, both receiving emotional and informational support increased thread initiators' satisfaction in general. However, if a thread initiator received support that did not match the type requested, this user's satisfaction decreased. In this work, we focus on whether previous messages will influence other responders' behavior in the ensuing conversation.

2 Measures

In this paper, we use *adaptation* measures at two levels, *linguistic* alignment and *pragmatic* similarity. Linguistic alignment quantifies by how much conversation participants adapt their language patterns to those of their interlocutors. Studies differ in the kinds of patterns examined: Some approaches measure linguistic adaptation using Linguistic Inquiry and Word Count (LIWC) (Tausczik and Pennebaker, 2010; Danescu-Niculescu-Mizil et al., 2011), and some focus on functional words (Jones et al., 2014). Other approaches measure repetition of words or syntactic rules (Church, 2000; Dubey et al., 2005; Fusaroli et al., 2012; Gries, 2005; Reitter et al., 2006). We use Indiscriminate Local Linguistic Alignment (Fusaroli et al., 2012) to measure linguistic alignment in this paper. Pragmatic similarity, for the purposes of the present study, evaluates the degree of matching social support types in conversation messages. In the following, we will introduce these measures.

2.1 Linguistic Alignment Measures

In this paper, we implement *Indiscriminate Local Linguistic Alignment* (Fusaroli et al., 2012) at lexical and syntactic levels to evaluate linguistic alignment. Generally, it measures the repetition of linguistic patterns among messages in the same conversation.

To be specific, *Lexical Indiscriminate Local Linguistic Alignment (LILLA)* measures word repetition between between pairs of messages (Wang et al., 2014; Fusaroli et al., 2012). The messages, ordered by occurrence in a thread of messages, will be called *prime post* and *target post*, respectively. In this study, they will sampled from the Cancer Support Network corpus. Formally, LILLA is calculated as

$$\text{LILLA}(target, prime) = \frac{\sum_{word_i \epsilon target} \delta(word_i)}{length(prime) * length(target)} \quad (1)$$

$$\delta(word_i) = \begin{cases} 1 & \text{if word}_i \ \epsilon \text{ prime} \\ 0 & otherwise \end{cases} \quad (2)$$

where *length(X)* is the number of words in post *X*.

We also measure syntactic alignment. Every sentence in each post is annotated with phrase structure trees using the Stanford CoreNLP parser (Klein and Manning, 2003). Each syntax tree is translated to a series of syntactic rules to encode the sequence of syntactic decisions. *Syntactic Indiscriminate Local Linguistic Alignment (SILLA)* is analogous to LILLA and measures repetition of syntactic rules between prime and target post pair, where *length(X)* in SILLA is the number of rules in post *X*. (Fusaroli et al., 2012; Wang et al., 2014).

2.2 Support Measures

As discussed above, emotional support and informational support are two most major support types in self support health communities (Wang et al., 2012; Rimer et al., 2005). Emotional support gives individual a feeling that s/he is cared for, or the facility of *"understanding/empathy, encouragement, affirmation/validation, sympathy, and caring/concern"* (Bambina, 2007). Emotional support does not include information. Here is an example of emotional support in CSN: *"I pray for you every night XXX.....and send you hugs and encouragement....you have the very BEST attitude and you must have a totally wonderful family. Love, XX"*

However, different from emotional support, informational support provides facts, advices and referrals (Bambina, 2007). Also, in our case, informational support only provides experience and information, without any emotional support. Another example of informational support in our data is: *"I am having similar problem with sacrum and hip, however not ready for biopsy in those areas. If you can tolerate pain waiting for new drugs to come will be beneficial. a new drug palbociclib (PD-0332991) expected to receive FDA approval in April of 2015"*.

In order to quantify the amount of one type of support in a reply post, we quantify the amount of one type of support (i.e. informational support, emotional support) in a comment post as *support index* Biyani et al. (2014), as follows: $Index_{type} = num_{type}/num_{classified}$, which is the proportion of sentences of a specific type in a post.

We will predict the emotional support index, $Index_{emo} = 1 - Index_{info}$ (for presentational reasons). The measure is produced automatically using the previously published classifier (Biyani et al., 2014).

3 Data Description

The data we use in this paper is from Cancer Survivor's Network (CSN) (`csn.cancer.org`), which is the largest active online community for cancer survivors. The CSN contains more than 166,000 users and 41 sub-communities (Portier et al., 2013). Users in one sub-community have experienced the same primary disease, similar health issues, surgeries. Furthermore, many users express depression. Most of the discussions in CSN are goal-directed and support-oriented conversations, which attracted our attention. Users would like to exchange their experiences and emotions in facing these tough situations.

We used threads from two largest sub-forums in the CSN: Breast cancer and Colorectal cancer. These sub-forums contain posts from the period of June 2000 to October 2010. The majority of posts in the breast cancer sub-forum are from female members, while most posts in the colorectal cancer sub-forum were authored by male patients. Thus, the two corpora are from relatively distinct, but representative user groups.

Mirroring the structure of other online communities, we refer to an initial post followed by a sequence of reply post as a *thread*. We treat the structure of these threads as a sequence of plain texts in temporal order, as members often use a general "reply" button to initiate replies, even when such messages are direct replies to a post. Thus, more detailed post relationships within each thread are sparse and not very reliable. A discussion thread is represented as a sequence of posts, $< P_0, P_1, \cdots, P_i, \cdots, P_n >$, where P_0 is called *initial post*, P_1 is called the *first reply of one thread* (simply called *first reply*) and the author of initial post is called the *thread initiator*. In most cases, the rest of replies provide help and emotional support to the thread initiator. The variable i is called the *absolute position* of post P_i. Posts in which the thread initiator replies to his or her message are excluded (as thread initiator may not provide support to themselves). The number of replies in a thread (without the initial post) is called the *length* of that thread. Both sub-communities have similar distributions of thread length. 90% of threads in Breast Cancer forum and Colorectal Cancer forum are shorter than 23 and 19, respectively.

We used a binary sentence classifier described by Biyani et al. (2014), which classifies sentences as providing either emotional or informational support. The classifier was trained in that work on more than 1,000 hand-annotated sentences; annotators reached 89% initial agreement. The classifier uses a variety of features, including subjective and cancer-related words, part-of-speech, phrases indicating support types. It yields an F-measure of 0.840.

4 Method

We treat the first reply of a thread as the prime, and each following reply as a target; thus, we include several prime-target data points per thread.

Table 1: Data Distribution in Breast Cancer and Colorectal Cancer sub-forums in CSN

	# of Users	# of Threads	# of Comments	# of Comment Pairs	% of Users who have posted in both forums
Breast Cancer	4,290	14,061	153,160	139,444	2.66%
Colorectal Cancer	2,348	13,282	125,527	112,602	4.85%

To address our first and second research questions, we fit a generalized linear mixed effects regression model with binominal kernel to predict the support index of a reply post given lexical and syntactical alignment measures, the support index in the first reply, post distance, number of sentences of that post and interactions terms among predictors in the thread. All the predictors in the model have been rescaled (but not centered).

4.1 Covariates

As a reminder, the model predicts the support index of a reply post (response variable) as a function of the following variables and interaction terms based on the previous work Wang et al. (2014). While the predicted informational support level is the sum of all predictors, pragmatic alignment is indicated as a positive correlation between the first reply's information support index and the response variable (see Table 3).

First Reply Support Index: This variable measures the proportion of informational support sentences in the post. A positive estimate (β) would indicate positive correlation of support type between the posts.

Post Distance: The distance between the data point (current post) and first reply in the thread can be seen as a proxy for how much information has been discussed so far in this thread, or for how much time has elapsed between the posts. A large post distance indicates that a post is far away from the initial post. Distance is measured in number of posts, as this is the most informative number: dates and times are not indicative of when a member has actually read the posts. Distance is interesting in our context, as the priming effect decays rapidly, as shown previously for the case of this corpus (Wang et al., 2014).

Linguistic Alignment: As discussed in the previous section, we use two linguistic alignment measures, Linguistic Alignment (LILLA) and Syntactic Alignment (SILLA) to link the linguistic to support index. This main effect helps us address the second research question.

Number of Sentences: This variable approximates the complexity and the amount of information in a given post.

Interaction terms between first reply Support Index and Post Distance: The distance effect on pragmatic alignment would indicate a decay effect which is similar to decay previous observations for linguistic repetition (Reitter et al., 2006).

Interaction terms between first reply Support Index and Linguistic Alignment Measurement: To address our second research question, we measure the correlation between linguistic alignment and support matching.

Interaction terms between Linguistic Alignment and Post Distance: These two interaction terms evaluate a correlation between linguistic decay and support index, which follows the IAM's cascade of alignment effects at different representational levels.

4.2 Experimental Settings

We treat predicting online social support as a generalized mixed effects linear regression with binomial kernel (e.g., Jaeger, 2008). Compared to other black-box machine learning algorithms, such as SVM, this model is directly interpretable. It predicts the probability of a message being emotional/informational support message using logit-link kernel. In this regression model, we also consider the effect of different threads. This is of concern because social support types in different posts influenced by various topics and authors of initial posts. Therefore, we employ a logistic

Table 2: Model performance of full model and drop one feature off model. Numbers in bold shows the best performing feature set.

Dataset	Breast Cancer Sub Forum			Colorectal Cancer Sub Forum		
Predictor	pseudo R-sq	AIC	BIC	pseudo R-sq	AIC	BIC
- first reply Info Support Index	11.19%	61838	61912	14.53%	49514	49586
- PostDistance	18.29%	58658	58732	27.93%	46987	47060
- Lexical Alignment	10.84%	59060	59142	10.52%	47519	47601
- Syntactic Alignment	20.46%	58633	58717	28.78%	46943	47026
- # of Sentence in the current post	19.63%	58898	59000	**29.63%**	47111	47211
- Lexical Alignment × first reply Info Support Index	15.95%	58836	58938	28.97%	46889	46997
- Syntactic Alignment × first reply Info Support Index	19.55%	58695	58796	28.27%	46844	46944
- first reply Info Support Index × Post Distance	21.34%	58750	58851	29.40%	46963	47063
- Lexical Alignment × Post-Distance	18.96%	58513	58614	29.39%	46883	46983
- Syntactic Alignment × Post-Distance	17.99%	58633	58735	28.93%	**46664**	**46763**
Full Model	**21.82%**	**58511**	**58622**	28.58%	46774	46882

regression model with random effects, grouped by *ThreadID*.

We use the lme4 R package (Bates et al., 2014). To evaluate the performance of drop one feature off models, we give conditional pseudo R-squared (pseudo R-sq), Akaike Information Criterion (AIC) and Bayesian Information Criterion (BIC) (Burnham and Anderson, 2002). The conditional R squared shows the proportion of variance explained (Barto, 2014, using R package MuMIN). AIC and BIC are measures of the quality of logistic regression model of current dataset.

All results reported in Table 2 are produced from 10 random sub-sampling validation with 70% training and 30% testing splits of threads.

4.3 Experiment Results

Table 3 reports effect sizes and directions, and Table 2 gives the performance of the informational support index prediction using generalized mixed effects linear regression model with binomial kernel. In Table 2, it shows the pseudo R-squared, AIC and BIC of models for different set of features and the full model.[1]

Overall, the full model which considers all the features we have listed out-performs other models. From the proportion of explained variable perspective (R-squared), it shows that the linguistic alignment and informational support index of the first reply are the two most important predictors, and increase a relatively larger proportion of variance explained in the model. Also, interaction terms considerably improve the model performance.

We rebuilt the model using the whole dataset in order to show and interpret effects of different predictors. The estimates and associated p-values given in Table 3 pertain to the two best models, predicting informational support index separately for the two sub-forums.

5 Discussion

Initially, we focus on the effect of the first reply support index addressing research question 1, whether online support provided by early responders

[1] We use the AIC scores to select the best generalized mixed effects linear regression model with binomial kernel, since AIC score evaluates the model based on both goodness of fit and model complexity (Burnham and Anderson, 2002).

Table 3: **Predicting Information Support Index** with generalized mixed effects linear regression models with binomial kernel, fitted to data from Breast Cancer and Colorectal Cancer Sub-Communities.

Dataset	Breast Cancer Sub Forum			Colorectal Cancer Sub Forum		
Predictor	beta	SE	p	beta	SE	p
Intercept	-1.552	0.022	0.000	-1.545	0.023	0.000
first reply Info Support Index	1.295	0.045	0.000	1.204	0.048	0.000
PostDistance	-0.351	0.051	0.000	-0.253	0.057	0.000
Lexical Alignment	-29.369	2.180	0.000	-47.786	2.588	0.000
Syntactic Alignment	0.989	0.266	0.000	0.861	0.276	0.001
# of Sentence in the current post	7.464	0.243	0.000	5.426	0.169	0.000
Lexical Alignment × first reply Info Support Index	58.150	3.592	0.000	73.163	4.410	0.000
Syntactic Alignment × first reply Info Support Index	0.433	0.655	0.509	-0.084	0.806	0.917
Post Distance × first reply Info Support Index	-0.114	0.113	0.310	-0.244	0.128	0.057
Lexical Alignment × Post-Distance	-23.346	6.080	0.000	-20.691	7.108	0.004
Syntactic Alignment × Post-Distance	0.256	0.702	0.715	0.181	0.807	0.823

influences the support index of replies from later responders. According to the regression models in Table 3, the support index of the first reply is positively correlated with the support indices of the later replies in both datasets. In short, people align at the pragmatic level when it comes to overall communicative intent. The intent of the first reply is matched by the intent shown in future replies.

Similar to linguistic alignment effects, we also consider the post distance effect. Previous studies (Reitter et al., 2006) showed that strong syntactic adaptation diminishes in seconds in spoken dialogue corpora. This phenomenon also has been found for individual syntactic constructions in written and spoken language (see Pickering and Ferreira, 2008, for a review) and also in dialogues in online communities (Wang et al., 2014). In order to test and measure the effect of early messages on later messages, we examine whether support index has the same characteristic. There are two components to an answer. First, the regression model (Table 3) suggests that informational support index generally decreases by post distance. In other words, less informational support is given as discussions proceed. It is worthwhile to note that conversations shift towards emotional support in this support-oriented community. Does alignment decay by distance? This answer is given by the interaction between distance and support index of the first reply. Evidence for such decay is weak: we have no support for decay in the Breast Cancer case, and some decay ($\beta = -0.244, p = 0.057$) in the Colorectal Cancer forum.

Another notable result is how linguistic and pragmatic alignment interact. The LILLA measure quantifies lexical adaptation between messages. Lexical alignment is reliably indicative of emotional support (negative information support) in both forums. The reasons for this correlation may be found in properties of informational support in both datasets. Informational support provided at a later time is likely to include new information, introducing new words. Emotional support, on the other hand, implies more consistent word choice. Syntactic adaptation (SILLA) shows no effect of syntactic alignment on support index.

To address our second initial question, we also evaluate the relationship of linguistic and pragmatic alignment using interaction terms between Linguistic Alignment and first reply

Support Index. From a theoretical perspective and previous empirical results, we expect to see that adaptation is consistent across different linguistic choices: it may be due to a cascade of priming effects and joint situational understanding (Garrod and Pickering, 2009), joint languages (Fusaroli et al., 2012), and/or a cognitive (memory) process that is common to the different choices (Reitter et al., 2011). We find a strong positive interaction between lexical alignment and Informational Support Index in the first reply. This means that when first-reply (prime) and other-reply (target) align in terms of their kinds of social support, then they also tend to show much more lexical alignment. The same cannot be said for the syntactic level.

Linguistic adaptation is correlated with high-level alignment. In order to validate this theoretical effect on our corpora, we observe interaction effects between lexical alignment and the support type alignment. We caution the reader, however, that this interaction effect is expected given that our measure of support type is a function not least of word choices. Thus, these predictors are by no means independent. However, as stated before, lexical alignment also correlates with stronger emotional support. The interaction effect of lexical alignment and post distance, present in both datasets, suggests that in later portions of each thread, lexical alignment is no longer predictive of such emotional support.

To summarize, the observations of main effects suggest that the type of support provided by early responders on the thread positively influences the type of support provided by later responders in our data. That is, pragmatic adaptation based on support index exists in our data. Also, the observations provide clues that informational support messages are more likely to be provided at the beginning of the thread discussions.

Moreover, with regard to our research question 2, there is a correlation between some linguistic alignment measurements and support index. Naturally, *these results are observational*: taken by themselves, they suggest no causality. We make our argument solely because the hypotheses tested were motivated by theoretical predictions. Our results are compatible with a theoretical perspective that explains mutual understanding and successful communication as being aided by a cascade of priming or language adaptation effects (Pickering and Garrod, 2004).

6 Conclusion

Motivated by the large proportion of online social support in peer-to-peer support online communities, we quantify and predict online support in the thread-based conversations. In a regression model, we have considered multiple factors, such as previous messages, linguistic alignment, and complexity. The results point to alignment phenomena at a pragmatic level. Such alignment tends to coincide with alignment of word choices. Both of these results are, to our knowledge novel. The interpretation of our regression model is congruent with the interactive alignment theory (Pickering and Garrod, 2004).

From an applied perspective the models we fitted to the forum data could facilitate filters to display certain useful posts, or to improve ranking of search results after analyzing a specific users' needs (i.e. providing results with high informational support index for seeking informational support). We believe that it might help health communities to improve user experience.

7 Acknowledgement

This research was made possible by a collaboration agreement between Penn State and the American Cancer Society. The authors would like to thank Kenneth Portier and Greta E. Greer for preparing the CSN dataset. Also, the authors would like to thank Prakhar Biyani for providing the source code of sentence classifier as well as Prasenjit Mitra and Yang Xu for their helpful discussions.

References

Tim Althoff, Cristian Danescu-Niculescu-Mizil, and Dan Jurafsky. How to ask for a favor: A case study on the success of altruistic requests. *arXiv preprint arXiv:1405.3282*, 2014.

Lars Backstrom, Jon Kleinberg, Lillian Lee, and Cristian Danescu-Niculescu-Mizil. Characterizing and curating conversation threads: expansion, focus, volume, re-entry. In *Proceedings of the sixth ACM international conference on Web search and data mining*, pages 13–22. ACM, 2013.

Antonina Bambina. *Online social support: the interplay of social networks and computer-mediated communication*. Cambria press, 2007.

Kamil Barto. *MuMIn: Multi-model inference*, 2014. R package version 1.10.5.

Douglas Bates, Martin Maechler, Ben Bolker, and Steven Walker. *lme4: Linear mixed-effects models using Eigen and S4*, 2014. R package version 1.1-7.

Kirsten Bergmann and Stefan Kopp. Gestural alignment in natural dialogue. In *Proceedings of the 34th Annual Conference of the Cognitive Science Society (CogSci 2012)*, 2012.

Prakhar Biyani, Cornelia Caragea, Prasenjit Mitra, and John Yen. Identifying emotional and informational support in online health communities. In *Proceedings of COLING 2014, the 25th International Conference on Computational Linguistics: Technical Papers*, pages 827–836, Dublin, Ireland, August 2014. Dublin City University and Association for Computational Linguistics.

J Kathryn Bock. Syntactic persistence in language production. *Cognitive psychology*, 18(3):355–387, 1986.

Holly P Branigan, Martin J Pickering, and Alexandra A Cleland. Syntactic co-ordination in dialogue. *Cognition*, 75(2):B13–B25, 2000.

Ngot Bui, John Yen, and Vasant Honavar. Temporal causality of social support in an online community for cancer survivors. 2015.

Kenneth P Burnham and David R Anderson. *Model selection and multimodel inference: a practical information-theoretic approach*. Springer, 2002.

Justin Cheng, Cristian Danescu-Niculescu-Mizil, and Jure Leskovec. How community feedback shapes user behavior. In *Eighth International AAAI Conference on Weblogs and Social Media*, 2014.

Kenneth W Church. Empirical estimates of adaptation: the chance of two noriegas is closer to p/2 than p 2. In *Proceedings of the 18th conference on Computational linguistics*, pages 180–186. Association for Computational Linguistics, 2000.

Sheldon Cohen and Garth McKay. Social support, stress and the buffering hypothesis: A theoretical analysis. *Handbook of psychology and health*, 4:253–267, 1984.

Cristian Danescu-Niculescu-Mizil and Lillian Lee. Chameleons in imagined conversations: A new approach to understanding coordination of linguistic style in dialogs. In *Proceedings of the 2nd Workshop on Cognitive Modeling and Computational Linguistics*, pages 76–87. Association for Computational Linguistics, 2011.

Cristian Danescu-Niculescu-Mizil, Michael Gamon, and Susan Dumais. Mark my words!: linguistic style accommodation in social media. In *Proceedings of the 20th international conference on World Wide Web*, pages 745–754. ACM, 2011.

Amit Dubey, Frank Keller, and Patrick Sturt. Parallelism in coordination as an instance of syntactic priming: Evidence from corpus-based modeling. In *Proceedings of the Human Language Technology Conference and the Conference on Empirical Methods in Natural Language Processing*, pages 827–834, Vancouver, Canada, 2005.

Michael C Frank and Noah D Goodman. Predicting pragmatic reasoning in language games. *Science*, 336 (6084):998–998, 2012.

Riccardo Fusaroli, Bahador Bahrami, Karsten Olsen, Andreas Roepstorff, Geraint Rees, Chris Frith, and Kristian Tylén. Coming to terms quantifying the benefits of linguistic coordination. *Psychological Science*, 23(8):931–939, 2012.

Simon Garrod and Anthony Anderson. Saying what you mean in dialogue: A study in conceptual and semantic coordination. *Cognition*, 27:181–218, 1987.

Simon Garrod and Martin J Pickering. Joint action, interactive alignment, and dialog. *Topics in Cognitive Science*, 1(2):292–304, 2009.

Stefan Th. Gries. Syntactic priming: A corpus-based approach. *Journal of Psycholinguistic Research*, 34 (4):365–399, 2005.

David Huffaker, Joseph Jorgensen, Francisco Iacobelli, Paul Tepper, and Justine Cassell. Computational measures for language similarity across time in online communities. In *Proceedings of the HLT-NAACL 2006 Workshop on Analyzing Conversations in Text and Speech*, pages 15–22. Association for Computational Linguistics, 2006.

T. Florian Jaeger. Categorical data analysis: Away from anovas (transformation or not) and towards logit mixed models. *Journal of Memory and Language*, 59(4): 434–446, 2008.

T. Florian Jaeger and Neal Snider. Implicit learning and syntactic persistence: Surprisal and cumulativity. *University of Rochester Working Papers in the Language Sciences*, 3(1):26–44, 2007.

Simon Jones, Rachel Cotterill, Nigel Dewdney, Kate Muir, and Adam Joinson. Finding zelig in text: A measure for normalising linguistic accommodation. In *25th International Conference on Computational Linguistics*. University of Bath, 2014.

Dan Klein and Christopher D Manning. Fast exact inference with a factored model for natural language parsing. *Advances in Neural Information Processing Systems*, pages 3–10, 2003.

Catherine Penny Hinson Langford, Juanita Bowsher, Joseph P Maloney, and Patricia P Lillis. Social support: a conceptual analysis. *Journal of advanced nursing*, 25(1):95–100, 1997.

Christine Kerres Malecki and Michelle Kilpatrick Demaray. What type of support do they need? investigating student adjustment as related to emotional, informational, appraisal, and instrumental support. *School Psychology Quarterly*, 18(3):231, 2003.

Martin J Pickering and Victor S Ferreira. Structural priming: a critical review. *Psychological Bulletin*, 134 (3):427, 2008.

Martin J. Pickering and Simon Garrod. Toward a mechanistic psychology of dialogue. *Behavioral and Brain Sciences*, 27:169–225, 2004.

Kenneth Portier, Greta E Greer, Lior Rokach, Nir Ofek, Yafei Wang, Prakhar Biyani, Mo Yu, Siddhartha Banerjee, Kang Zhao, Prasenjit Mitra, and John Yen. Understanding topics and sentiment in an online cancer survivor community. *JNCI Monographs*, 2013 (47):195–198, 2013.

Baojun Qiu, Kang Zhao, Prasenjit Mitra, Dinghao Wu, Cornelia Caragea, John Yen, Greta E Greer, and Kenneth Portier. Get online support, feel better–sentiment analysis and dynamics in an online cancer survivor community. In *Privacy, Security, Risk and Trust (PASSAT) and 2011 IEEE Third Inernational Conference on Social Computing (SocialCom), 2011 IEEE Third International Conference on*, pages 274–281. IEEE, 2011.

David Reitter and Johanna D Moore. Predicting success in dialogue. In *Annual Meeting of the Association for Computational Linguistics*, volume 45, page 808, 2007.

David Reitter and Johanna D. Moore. Alignment and task success in spoken dialogue. *Journal of Memory and Language*, 76:29–46, 2014.

David Reitter, Johanna D. Moore, and Frank Keller. Priming of syntactic rules in task-oriented dialogue and spontaneous conversation. In *Proceedings of the 28th Annual Conference of the Cognitive Science Society (CogSci)*, pages 685–690, Vancouver, Canada, 2006.

David Reitter, Frank Keller, and Johanna D. Moore. A computational cognitive model of syntactic priming. *Cognitive Science*, 35(4):587–637, 2011.

Barbara K Rimer, Elizabeth J Lyons, Kurt M Ribisl, J Michael Bowling, Carol E Golin, Michael J Forlenza, and Andrea Meier. How new subscribers use cancer-related online mailing lists. *Journal of medical internet research*, 7(3), 2005.

Lauren E Scissors, Alastair J Gill, and Darren Gergle. Linguistic mimicry and trust in text-based cmc. In *Proceedings of the 2008 ACM Conference on Computer Supported Cooperative Work*, pages 277–280. ACM, 2008.

Yla R Tausczik and James W Pennebaker. The psychological meaning of words: Liwc and computerized text analysis methods. *Journal of language and social psychology*, 29(1):24–54, 2010.

Tatiana A Vlahovic, Yi-Chia Wang, Robert E Kraut, and John M Levine. Support matching and satisfaction in an online breast cancer support community. In *Proceedings of the 32nd annual ACM conference on Human factors in computing systems*, pages 1625–1634. ACM, 2014.

Yafei Wang, David Reitter, and John Yen. Linguistic adaptation in online conversation threads: Analyzing alignment in online health communities. In *Proceedings of the Fifth Workshop on Cognitive Modeling and Computational Linguistics*, pages 55–62, Baltimore, Maryland, USA, June 2014. Association for Computational Linguistics.

Yi-Chia Wang, Robert Kraut, and John M Levine. To stay or leave?: the relationship of emotional and informational support to commitment in online health support groups. In *Proceedings of the ACM 2012 conference on Computer Supported Cooperative Work*, pages 833–842. ACM, 2012.

Kang Zhao, John Yen, Greta Greer, Baojun Qiu, Prasenjit Mitra, and Kenneth Portier. Finding influential users of online health communities: a new metric based on sentiment influence. *Journal of the American Medical Informatics Association*, pages amiajnl–2013, 2014.

Audience size and contextual effects on information density in Twitter conversations

Gabriel Doyle
Dept. of Psychology
Stanford University
Stanford, CA, USA, 94305
gdoyle@stanford.edu

Michael C. Frank
Dept. of Psychology
Stanford University
Stanford, CA, USA, 94305
mcfrank@stanford.edu

Abstract

The "uniform information density" (UID) hypothesis proposes that language producers aim for a constant rate of information flow within a message, and research on monologue-like written texts has found evidence for UID in production. We consider conversational messages, using a large corpus of tweets, and look for UID behavior. We do not find evidence of UID behavior, and even find context effects that are opposite that of previous, monologue-based research. We propose that a more collaborative conception of information density and careful consideration of channel noise may be needed in the information-theoretic framework for conversation.

1 Introduction

Linguistic communication can be viewed from an information theoretic standpoint as communication via a noisy channel. If humans are approximately rational in their communications and the noisy channel model is appropriate, then we expect to see communication follow an approximately constant rate of information flow. This is the Uniform Information Density (UID) hypothesis.

Evidence in favor of UID has been found in many levels of language production. At the level of within-sentence context, there is clear evidence from phonology that speakers reduce more predictable sounds (Aylett and Turk, 2004; Aylett and Turk, 2006; Bell et al., 2003; Demberg et al., 2012), suggesting that they are giving more "air time" to less predictable material to equalize information density. And in syntax, speakers tend to drop optional materials (like the word "that" as a sentence-complementizer) in more predictable scenarios (Levy and Jaeger, 2007; Frank and Jaeger, 2008; Jaeger, 2010), again implying a process of allocating communication time relative to predictability. These effects appear in both monologues and dialogues, suggesting that local linguistic context shapes message complexity.

There is also some evidence for UID based on broader, discourse-level context. Genzel and Charniak (2002) showed that word-by-word complexity (measured by a standard n-gram language model) increases across sequences of sentences. They hypothesized that this increase was due to a corresponding increase in non-linguistic information that would make even more complex linguistic structures easier to predict. Follow-ups have shown that this same complexity increase effect is attested in different document types and across languages (Genzel and Charniak, 2003; Qian and Jaeger, 2012). However, these studies draw almost exclusively from long, well-structured written texts that function as monologues from writer to reader.

This leaves an important gap in these tests of the UID hypothesis: little work has looked at the influence of discourse-level context on information structure in interpersonal dialogue, the archetype of human linguistic communication. With the exception of one preliminary study that provided a partial replication of the original complexity increase effect using the Switchboard corpus (Vega and Ward, 2009), to our knowledge no work has explored how the broader dynamics of conversation interact with UID.

Proceedings of CMCL 2015, pages 19–28,
Denver, Colorado, June 4, 2015.

The present study applies information-theoretic analysis to a corpus of social media microblog posts that include a large number of natural dialogues. Surprisingly, we do not see clear evidence of the UID hypothesis in these dialogues. Instead, we propose that differences in the discourse-level structure of conversation compared to monologues, such as the desire to establish that mutual understanding has been reached, may interfere with attaining UID in the standard formulation. A more collaborative view of UID, encompassing content generation and grounding (Clark and Schaefer, 1987), may be needed to fully represent conversational structure.

1.1 Conversations, context, and content

One common motivation for the UID hypothesis is a rational analysis based on a noisy-channel model of communication (Levy and Jaeger, 2007).[1] In the noisy-channel analysis, the amount of noise in the channel sets an optimal value for information density to obtain fast, error-free transmission. For a noise level α, we will refer to the optimal information content per discourse unit Y_i as $H_\alpha(Y_i)$. Discourse units, depending on the analysis, range from syllables to whole documents; in our analyses, we focus on words and tweets as our discourse units.

In the course of a message, as argued by Genzel and Charniak (2002), the actual information content per discourse unit is predicted by the entropy of the random variable X_i representing the precise word choice or choices within the discourse unit, conditioned on the available context. The precise extent of this context is difficult to pin down.

We estimate context for our studies by thinking in terms of the *common ground* that a rational speaker believes to exist, given the expected audience of their message. Common ground is defined as the knowledge that participants in a discourse have and that participants know other participants have, including the current conversational context (Clark, 1996). This common ground can be built from a combination of linguistic and non-linguistic context, including previous messages within the discourse, preceding interactions between the conversation participants, and world knowledge.

[1]The other common motivation is a surprisal-based argument (Levy, 2008): maintaining UID also minimizes the listener's comprehension effort.

To formalize this relationship, let C_i be the common ground that exists prior to the production of discourse unit Y_i, and let α be the expected noise level in the channel that Y_i is transmitted through. Then optimality within a noisy channel model predicts that the noise-dependent optimal information rate $H_\alpha(Y_i)$ is related to the actual information rate as follows:

$$H_\alpha(Y_i|C_i) = H(X_i) - I(X_i;C_i) \quad (1)$$

Here, $H(X_i)$ is the apparent decontextualized entropy of the discourse unit independent of the common ground. This quantity is often estimated from a language model that uses only local context, not higher-level discourse context or common ground. We use a trigram Markov model in this study.

$I(X_i;C_i)$ is the mutual information of the discourse unit random variable X_i and the common ground C_i—essentially how much more predictable the next discourse unit becomes from knowing the common ground. Common ground is difficult to quantify—both in the particular datasets we consider and more generally—so we rely on the assumption that more common ground is correlated with greater mutual information, as in Genzel and Charniak (2002).

Then, based on this assumption, Eq. 1 allows us to make two UID-based predictions. First, as channel noise increases, transmission error should increase, which in turn should cause the optimal information transfer rate $H_\alpha(Y_i)$ to decrease. Thus, to maintain equality with rising noise, the apparent entropy $H(X_i)$ should decrease. This prediction translates into communicators "slowing down" their speech (albeit in terms of information per word, rather than per unit time) to account for increased errors.

Second, as common ground increases, $I(X_i;C_i)$ should increase. To maintain equality with rising common ground, $H(X_i)$ should thus also increase, so as not to convey information slower than necessary. This prediction translates into communicators "going faster" (e.g., packing more information into each word) because of an assumption that listeners share more common ground with them.

1.2 The current study

We take advantage of the conversational structure of the popular social media microblogging platform Twitter (`http://twitter.com`) to test these predictions. Twitter allows users to post 140 character "tweets" in a number of different conversational contexts. In particular, because some tweets are replies to previous tweets, we can use this reply structure to build conversational trees, and to track the number of participants. In addition, specific choices in tweet production can affect what audience is likely to see the tweet. These variables are discussed in depth in Section 2.2.

To test the entropy effects predicted by Eq. 1, we first examine different types of tweets that reach different audience sizes. We then restrict our analysis to reply tweets with varying audience sizes to analyze audience size independently of noise. Finally, we look at the effects of common ground (by way of conversation structure) on tweet entropy. Contrary to previous UID findings, we do not see a clear increase in apparent entropy estimates due to more extensive common ground, as had been found in previous non-conversational work (Genzel and Charniak, 2002; Qian and Jaeger, 2012; Doyle and Frank, 2015).

We propose two factors that may be influencing conversational content in addition to UID factors. First, achieving conversational goals may be more dependent on certain discourse units that carry low linguistic informativity but substantial social/conversational importance. Second, considering and adapting to two different types of noise—message loss and message corruption—may cause tweeters to make large-scale decisions that overwhelm UID effects.

2 Corpus

Randomly sampling conversations on a medium like Twitter is a difficult problem. Twitter users routinely use the medium to converse in smaller groups via the mention functionality (described in more detail below). Yet such conversations are not uniformly distributed: A random sample of tweets—perhaps chosen because they contain the word "the" or a similarly common token (Doyle, 2014)—yields mostly isolated tweets rather than complete dialogues. Dialogues depend on users interacting back and forth within communities.

Seed Users	Category
@camerondallas @rickypdillon	Youtube stars
@edsheeran @yelyahwilliams	Musicians
@felixsalmon @tanehisicoates	Journalists
@jahimes @jaredpolis @leezeldin	Politicians
@larrymishel @paulnvandewater	Economists
@neiltyson @profbriancox @richardwiseman	Scientists

Table 1: Seed users for our dataset.

2.1 Seed strategy

To sample such interactions, we developed a "seed" strategy where we identified popular Twitter accounts and then downloaded a large sample of their tweets, then downloaded a sample of the tweets of all the users they mentioned. This strategy allowed us to reconstruct a relatively dense sample of dialogues (reply chains).

We began by choosing a set of 14 seed Twitter accounts (Table 1) that spanned a variety of genres, were popular enough to elicit replies, and interacted with other users often enough to build up a community.

To build conversations, we needed to obtain tweets directed to and from these seed users. For each seed user, we downloaded their last 1500 tweets, extracted all users mentioned within those tweets, and downloaded each of their last 1500 tweets. To capture tweets that failed to start conversations with the seed users, we also added the last 1000 tweets mentioning each seed user's handle. Tweets that appeared in multiple communities were removed. Each reply contains the ID of the tweet it replies to, so we could rebuild conversation trees back to their roots, so long as all of the preceding tweets were made by users in our communities.

2.2 Conversation structure and visibility

Twitter conversations follow a basic tree structure with a unique root node. Each tweet is marked as a reply or not; for replies, the user and tweet IDs of the tweet it replies to is stored. Each tweet can be a reply to at most one other tweet, so a long conversation resembles a linked list with a unique root node. "Mentions," the inclusion of a username in a tweet, are included in tweets by default throughout a conversation unless a tweeter chooses to remove some of them, so tweets deep in a conversation may be primarily composed of mentions rather than new information.

After some processing described below, our sampling process resulted in 5.5 million tweets, of which 3.3 million were not part of a conversation (not a reply, and received no replies). Within this data, we found 63,673 conversations that could be traced back to a root tweet, spanning 228,923 total tweets. Unfortunately, Twitter only tracks replies up a tree, so while we know with certainty whether a tweet is a reply (even if it is to a user outside our communities), we do not know with certainty that a tweet has received no replies, especially from users outside our communities. If anything, this fact makes our analyses conservative, as they may understate differences between reply and non-reply tweets. The remaining 2 million tweets were replies whose conversations could not be traced back to the root.

2.3 Information content estimation

To estimate the information content of a tweet, we first tokenized the tweets using Twokenizer (Owoputi et al., 2013). We then removed any number of mentions at the beginning or end of a tweet, as these are usually used to address certain users rather than to convey information themselves. (Tweets that only contained mentions were removed.) Tweet-medial mentions were retained but masked with the single type *[MENTION]* to reduce sparsity. Links were similarly masked as *[URL]*. Punctuation and emoji were retained. We then built trigram language models using SRILM with default settings and Kneser-Ney discounting. Types with fewer than 5 tokens were treated as out-of-vocabulary items.

For each community, the training set was the set of all tweets from all other communities. This training set provides tweets that are contemporaneous to the test set and cover some of the same topics without containing the same users' tweets.

3 Analyses

We describe the results of three sets of analyses looking at the influence of audience size and available context on apparent tweet entropy. The first examines the effect of expected audience size at a coarse level, comparing tweets directed at a small subset of users, all one's followers, or the wider realm of a hashtag. The second examines the effect of finer differences in known audience size on apparent informativity. The third examines the effects of conversational context and length on informativity.

3.1 Expected audience size

First, we consider three different types of tweets and their expected audience size. Tweets whose first character is a mention (whether or not it is a reply) do not show up by default when browsing a user's tweets, unless the browser follows both the tweeter and first-mentioned user.[2] We will refer to these as "invisible" tweets as they are invisible to followers by default. A tweeter making an initial-mention tweet thus should expect such a tweet to have a relatively limited audience, with a focus on the mentioned users.[3]

On the other side, a hashtag serves as a categorization mechanism so that interested users can discover new content. Hashtags are often used to expand the potential audience for a tweet to include the feeds of users tracking that hashtag, regardless of whether they follow the original tweeter, and so a tweeter using a hashtag should expect a larger audience than

[2]This behavior varies slightly depending on what application is used to view Twitter. On the website, mention-first tweets do not appear in lists and only appear after clicking the 'tweets & replies' option on a timeline. On the Twitter mobile app, mention-first tweets appear by default on a timeline but still not in lists.

[3]Some Twitter users consciously manipulate audience using these markers: many tweets have an initial period or other punctuation mark to prevent it from being hidden. Some users routinely switch between initial-mention replies and "dot"-replies in the course of a conversation to change the audience, presumably depending on their estimate of the wider relevance of a remark.

Type	Tweet	Per-word entropy
invisible	[MENTION] [MENTION] this is so accurate tho	6.00
	[MENTION] can you come to my high school ? ;3	7.61
	[MENTION] Hi Kerry , Please send us your email address in order to discuss this matter further . Thanks !	8.58
baseline	post your best puns in the comments of my latest instagram photo : [URL]	7.44
	I wish I could start a blog dedicated to overly broad and sweeping introductory sentences	9.98
	this new year's eve in NYC , keep an eye peeled 4 Sad Michael Stipe . [URL] already found him : [URL]	7.17
hashtagged	I will probably be quitting my job when #GTAV comes out	7.63
	#UMAlumni what is the number one thing graduating seniors should know ? #MGoGrad	6.80
	Brilliant interactive infographic : shows cone of uncertainty for #climatechange [URL] #howhotwillitget	12.1

Table 2: Example tweets from each category.

normal.[4] Finally, we have baseline tweets which contain neither mentions nor hashtags and whose expected audience size is approximately one's followers.

Intuitively, common ground is higher for smaller audiences. It should be highest for the invisible tweets, where the audience is limited and has seen or can readily access the previous tweets in the conversation. It should be lowest for the hashtagged tweets, where the audience is the largest and will likely contain many users who are completely unfamiliar with the tweeter. If contextualized UID is the driving force affecting information content, then the invisible tweets should have the highest entropy and hashtagged tweets should have the lowest.

In this analysis, we use the full 5.5 million tweet database. Figure 1 plots the entropy of tweets for these three audience sizes. Per-word and per-tweet entropy both significantly *increase* with expected audience size ($p < .001$ by likelihood-ratio test), the opposite direction of our prediction. We discuss this finding below in the context of our next analyses.

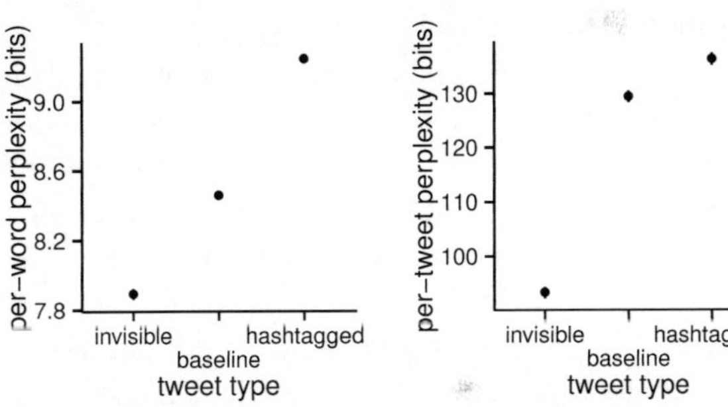

Figure 1: Per-word (left) and per-tweet (right) entropy are higher for tweets with larger expected audience size. Error bars (in some cases smaller than plotting marker) show by-user 95% confidence intervals.

3.2 Known audience size

The results from expected audience size in Section 3.1 have a potential explanation: different tweet types are received and viewed in different ways, which may encourage different kinds of communicative behavior. Tweets with mentions are highly likely to be seen by the mentioned user (unless the mentioned user is very popular), whereas the likelihood of a given hashtagged tweet being seen through the hashtag-searching mechanism is very low. This uncertainty about audience may lead a rational tweeter to package information into tweets differently: they may include more redundant information across tweets when the likelihood of any

[4] Not all hashtags are intended for categorization; some are used for emphasis or metalinguistic comment (e.g. #notmyfavoritefridaymeal, #toomuchinformation). These comments are probably not intended to broaden the tweet's audience. The presence of such hashtags should, if anything, cause our analysis to underestimate variability across audience types.

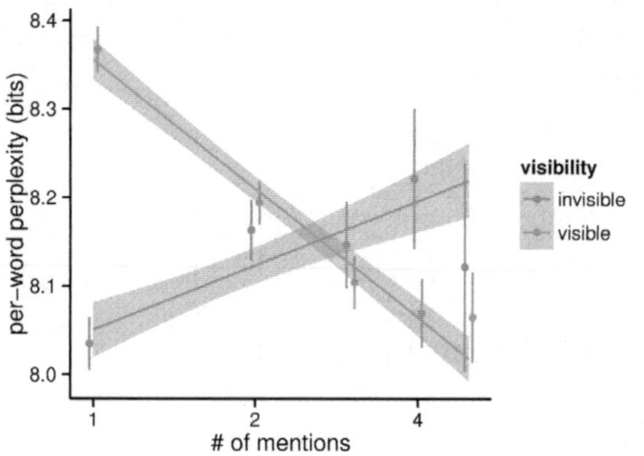

Figure 2: Per-word entropy of tweets with different numbers of mentions and different visibility. Invisible tweets' entropy increases with mentions, while visible tweets' entropy decreases. Logarithmic fits with 95% confidence intervals; x-axis is log-scaled.

given tweet being read is low.

To assess audience size effects in a more controlled setting, we look at invisible tweets with varying numbers of mentions. Invisible tweets provide a quantifiable audience size; those with few mentions have a smaller audience than those with more mentions. Visible tweets, on the other hand, have approximately the same audience size regardless of the number of mentions, since all of a user's followers can see them. Visible mentions can be used for a wide range of discourse functions (e.g., self-promotion, bringing one's followers into an argument, entering contests), and so we do not have a clear prediction of their behavior. But invisible mentions should, under the UID hypothesis, show decreased common ground as the number of conversation participants grows and it is harder to achieve consensus on what all participants know.

Figure 2 shows that the per-word entropy of invisible tweets goes up with the logarithm of the number of mentions. We look only at tweets with between one and five mentions, as invisible tweets must have at least one mention, and five mentions already substantially cut into the 140-character limit.[5] This leaves 1.4 million tweets.

The fact that invisible tweet entropy increases

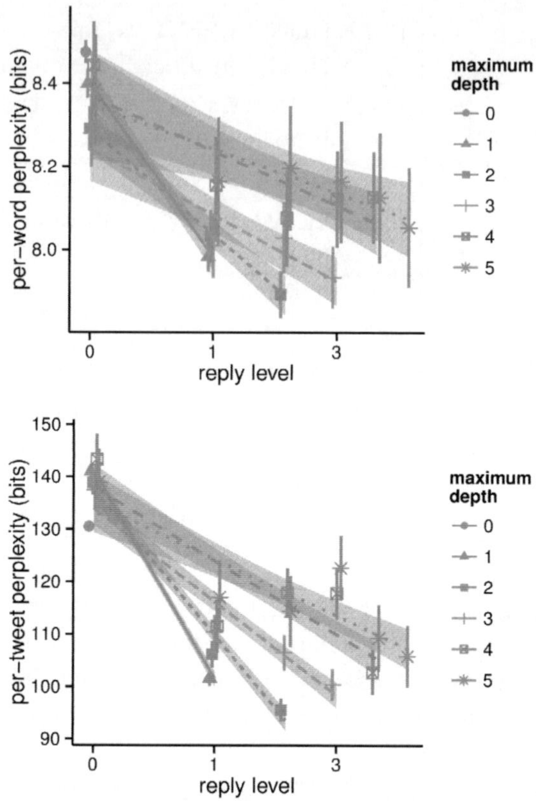

Figure 3: Per-word (top) and per-tweet (bottom) entropy decrease with reply level and increase with conversation length. Logarithmic fits with 95% confidence intervals; x-axis is log-scaled.

with number of mentions, even as visible tweet entropy decreases, suggests that audience size is having an effect. However, this effect is causing entropy to increase as common ground should be decreasing due to the larger number of conversation participants. Furthermore, this effect is not driven by reply level (Sect 3.3); there is a significant increase ($p < .001$) in explanatory power from adding number of mentions to a mixed-effects model with fixed-effects of reply level and a by-user random intercept.

3.3 Reply level and conversation length

We next turn to our second UID prediction: that information content should increase as common ground increases. As common ground is assumed to increase in dialogues (Clark, 1996), we thus predict that Twitter conversations should show increases in

[5]Usernames can be up to 15 characters (plus a space and an symbol per mention); even if each username is only 7 characters, five mentions use almost one-third of the character limit.

information content that scale with reply level, the number of replies between the current tweet and the conversation root. Such a result would constitute a replication of Genzel and Charniak (2002) in the discourse context, and would confirm preliminary results on the Switchboard corpus by Vega and Ward (2009). As is clear from our analysis below, that is not what we found.

Figure 3 plots mean perplexities for different reply levels and conversation lengths, with confidence intervals based on by-user means. Increasing the reply level decreases the information content of the tweet, while increasing the conversation length increases the information content.

We fit a linear mixed-effects regression model to per-word and per-tweet perplexity. Control factors were the logarithm of the tweet reply level and the logarithm of the conversation length, along with a separate binary variable for whether the tweet was part of a conversation at all, and random by-user intercepts. Both log reply level and log conversation length had significant effects by likelihood-ratio tests.

Log reply level had negative effects on per-word and per-tweet perplexity (per-word: $-.341 \pm .009$; per-tweet: $-39.6 \pm .3$; both $p < .001$). Log conversation length had positive effects on per-word and per-tweet perplexity (per-word: $.285 \pm .010$; per-tweet: $35.1 \pm .3$; both $p < .001$).

To summarize these effects, all conversations lose entropy as they go along, and tweets that start longer conversations tend to have higher entropy to start. Whereas previous work has suggested that messages become more unpredictable as context builds up, Twitter conversations appear to shift to more predictable messages as context builds up, and seem to go until messages get sufficiently predictable. We discuss these results below.

4 General Discussion

Previous work supports the UID hypothesis that rational communicators adjust their messages so as to spread information as uniformly as possible in response to local context (Aylett and Turk, 2004; Levy and Jaeger, 2007), as well as to discourse-level context in monologic writing (Genzel and Charniak, 2002; Qian and Jaeger, 2012).

Our current work synthesizes these two bodies of work by looking for evidence of discourse-level UID effects in a large corpus of Twitter conversations, including dialogues and many-party conversations. Contrary to expectations, we failed to find UID effects; in fact, we often found information rate *increasing* when context changes would have predicted decreasing information rates. Specifically, we found that messages to smaller audiences, which should have lower noise and greater context and hence higher information density, actually have *lower* information density than messages to larger, noisier, and less context-sharing audiences. Furthermore, we found that later messages within a reply chain, which should have greater context, have less information. This last result is especially surprising because UID context effects have been repeatedly found in less conversational texts.

So should we give up on UID? While our results were unexpected, as we discuss below, we believe that they instead encourage more reflection on how speakers conceptualize information for conversational UID. We consider two aspects of these conversations: first, that the collaborative nature of conversation introduces rational uses for messages with low (lexicosyntactic) information density; second, that rational behaviors resulting from the nature of noise in social media communication complicates our evaluations of UID.

4.1 Information in terms of contributions

Why do Twitter conversations look different from the increasingly-informative texts studied in previous work? For one, our dataset contains true conversations, whereas almost all of the sentence-level context informativity results were based on single-author texts.

In monologues, there is neither an ability nor a need to check that common ground has been established. Participants in a conversation, though, must both produce content and establish grounding (Clark and Schaefer, 1987). Participants employ many methods to establish grounding, including backchannels (Yngve, 1970; Schegloff, 1982; Iwasaki, 1997), which have little lexicosyntactic information but provide crucial turn-taking and grounding cues.

Dialogues are often reactive; for instance, a reply may be a clarification question, such as this reply in our dataset: *[MENTION] What do you mean you saw the pattern?* Such replies are typically shorter and more predictable than the original statement, and are often part of adjacency or coordinate pairs (Schegloff and Sacks, 1973; Clark and French, 1981), where one participant's utterance massively constrains the other's next utterance. Such pairs cover a wide range of low-entropy messages that are likely to appear in multi-party conversation but not in monologic text, including question-and-answers, offer-and-acceptances, and goodbyes.

As a result, Clark and Schaefer (1987) argue for a collaborative view of conversation structure, with conversations best viewed not as a series of utterances but as a series of contributions—sets of utterances that, combined, both specify some new content and establish it as part of the common ground. UID as a rational behavior is based on the idea that a rational speaker seeks to maximize linguistic information transfer, which would seem to be the primary goal during the content-specification portion of a contribution. During the grounding portion of a contribution, though, the primary goal is likely to be to establish common ground as quickly as possible. This goal is potentially more complex, as it depends on a variety of factors including the quality of the content-specification portion. If the content specification was simple and clear, grounding can be acheived with low-entropy backchannels (*mm-hmm, right*, etc.); if it was complex or unclear, grounding will require more messages and greater message entropy.

Furthermore, conversations may contain exchanges that have little linguistic context but serve important social ends. Many response tweets in our dataset are single, common words (*haha, lol*) or emoji/emoticons. These provide important emotional information in a very low lexicosyntactic entropy package, much as a backchannel or metalinguistic cue (e.g., a smile) might in face-to-face conversation. This suggests that the information measure within UID may not be strictly based on literal lexicosyntactic information but rather a combination of linguistic and metalinguistic information.

In sum, this conception suggests that in discourse, UID may operate as usual for parts of a contribution, but not necessarily throughout it. Rational conversational behavior may resemble an error-checking system in which UID may be observed at a contribution-by-contribution level.

4.2 Multiple types of noise

In most of the previously-studied genres, the authors of the texts could reasonably expect their readers to be both focused and unlikely to stop while reading. Tweets, however, are often read and responded to while doing other tasks, reducing focus and increasing disengagement rates. Interestingly, the one genre where Genzel and Charniak (2003) found a negative effect of sentence number on informativity was tabloid newspapers, where readers are likely to be distractable and disengaged.

It may be that Twitter requires an idiosyncratic adjustment to the noisy-channel model: perhaps the locus of the noise in tweets should not be in comprehension of the tweet per se (or at least not exclusively on comprehension). Instead, the main source of noise for Twitter users may be whether a reader engages with the tweet at all. Many Twitter users follow an enormous number of users, so outside of directed mentions and replies, there is a substantial chance that any given tweet will go unread by the larger part of its intended audience.[6]

The decreases we observed may have to do with users optimizing the amount of information content relative to the likelihood of an audience-member seeing more than one message. For tweets that go the largest audience, it is unlikely that multiple tweets would all be seen; thus it makes more sense to send information-rich tweets that can stand alone. In contrast, for replies, the intended audience should notice each sent tweet.

Evidence in favor of the conversation- or noise-based explanation could be obtained by comparing the Twitter reply chain effects against a corpus of conversations in which message reception is essentially certain, as in person-to-person chat logs (e.g., Potts 2012). If noise at the message level accounts for the anomalous Twitter behavior, then

[6]As a result, tweeters often create tweets that include their own context; for instance, a reply may quote part of its preceding tweet, or a user may talk about a recent event and include an explanatory link. This example from the corpus does both: *Pls help if you can! RT [MENTION]: Henry broke his foot [URL] Please donate: [URL].*

chat logs should show the UID effect of increasing entropy through the conversation. If turn-taking or meta-linguistic discourse functions drive it, chat logs would show decreasing entropy, as in our data.

4.3 Conclusions

We tested the Uniform Information Density hypothesis, which has been robustly demonstrated in monologue-like settings, on dialogues in Twitter. Surprisingly, we failed to find the predicted effects of context within these dialogues, and at times found evidence for effects going in the opposite direction. We proposed that this behavior may indicate a crucial difference in how information flow is structured between monologues and conversations, as well as how rational adaptation to noise manifests in different conversational settings.

Acknowledgments

We gratefully acknowledge the support of ONR Grant N00014-13-1-0287.

References

Matthew Aylett and Alice Turk. 2004. The smooth signal redundancy hypothesis: A functional explanation for relationships between redundancy, prosodic prominence, and duration in spontaneous speech. *Language and Speech*, 47(1):31–56.

Matthew Aylett and Alice Turk. 2006. Language redundancy predicts syllabic duration and the spectral characteristics of vocalic syllable nuclei. *The Journal of the Acoustical Society of America*, 119(5):3048–3058.

Alan Bell, Daniel Jurafsky, Eric Fosler-Lussier, Cynthia Girand, Michelle Gregory, and Daniel Gildea. 2003. Effects of disfluencies, predictability, and utterance position on word form variation in English conversation. *The Journal of the Acoustical Society of America*, 113(2):1001–1024.

Herbert H. Clark and J. Wade French. 1981. Telephone goodbyes. *Language in Society*, 10:1–19.

Herbert H. Clark and Edward F. Schaefer. 1987. Collaborating on contributions to conversations. *Language and Cognitive Processes*, 2:19–41.

Herbert H. Clark. 1996. *Using language*, volume 1996. Cambridge University Press Cambridge.

Vera Demberg, Asan Sayeed, Phillip Gorinski, and Nikolaos Engonopoulos. 2012. Syntactic surprisal affects spoken word duration in conversational contexts. In *Proceedings of the 2012 Joint Conference on Empirical Methods in Natural Language Processing and Computational Natural Language Learning*, pages 356–367.

Gabriel Doyle and Michael C. Frank. 2015. Shared common ground influences information density in microblog texts. In *Proceedings of NAACL-HLT*.

Gabriel Doyle. 2014. Mapping dialectal variation by querying social media. In *Proceedings of the European Chapter of the Association for Computational Linguistics*.

Austin Frank and T. Florian Jaeger. 2008. Speaking rationally: Uniform information density as an optimal strategy for language production. In *Proceedings of the 30th Annual Meeting of the Cognitive Science Society*, pages 933–938. Cognitive Science Society Washington, DC.

Dmitriy Genzel and Eugene Charniak. 2002. Entropy rate constancy in text. In *Proceedings of the 40th Annual Meeting of the Association for Computational Linguistics*, pages 199–206. Association for Computational Linguistics.

Dmitriy Genzel and Eugene Charniak. 2003. Variation of entropy and parse trees of sentences as a function of the sentence number. In *Proceedings of the 2003 conference on Empirical Methods in Natural Language Processing*, pages 65–72. Association for Computational Linguistics.

Shoichi Iwasaki. 1997. The northridge earthquake conversations: The floor structure and the 'loop' sequence in japanese conversation. *Jouranl of Pragmatics*, 28:661–693.

T. Florian Jaeger. 2010. Redundancy and reduction: Speakers manage syntactic information density. *Cognitive Psychology*, 61(1):23–62.

Roger Levy and T. Florian Jaeger. 2007. Speakers optimize information density through syntactic reduction. In *Advances in Neural Information Processing Systems*, pages 849–856.

Roger Levy. 2008. Expectation-based syntactic comprehension. *Cognition*, 106(3):1126–1177.

Olutobi Owoputi, Brendan O'Connor, Chris Dyer, Kevin Gimpel, Nathan Schneider, and Noah A. Smith. 2013. Improved part-of-speech tagging for online conversational text with word clusters. In *Proceedings of NAACL-HLT*.

Christopher Potts. 2012. Goal-driven answers in the Cards dialogue corpus. In Nathan Arnett and Ryan Bennett, editors, *Proceedings of the 30th West Coast Conference on Formal Linguistics*, Somerville, MA. Cascadilla Press.

Ting Qian and T. Florian Jaeger. 2012. Cue effectiveness in communicatively efficient discourse production. *Cognitive Science*, 36(7):1312–1336.

Emanuel Schegloff and Harvey Sacks. 1973. Opening up closings. *Semiotica*, 8:289–327.

Emanuel Schegloff. 1982. Discourse as an interactional achievement: Some uses of 'uh huh' and other things that come between sentences. In Deborah Tannen, editor, *Analyzing Discourse: Text and Talk*, pages 71–93. Georgetown Univ. Press.

Alejandro Vega and Nigel Ward. 2009. Looking for entropy rate constancy in spoken dialog. Technical Report UTEP-CS-09-19, UTEP.

Victor Yngve. 1970. On getting a word in edgewise. In *Papers from the Sixth Regional Meeting of the Chicago Linguistic Society*, pages 567–578. Univ. of Chicago Dept. of Linguistics.

Centre Stage:
How Social Network Position Shapes Linguistic Coordination

Bill Noble and **Raquel Fernández**
Institute for Logic, Language and Computation
University of Amsterdam
winobes@gmail.com, raquel.fernandez@uva.nl

Abstract

In conversation, speakers tend to echo the linguistic style of the person they are interacting with. This paper contributes to a body of work that addresses how this linguistic style coordination is affected by the social context in which the interaction occurs. In particular, we investigate the effect that an agent's social network centrality has on the coordination exhibited in replies to their utterances. We find that linguistic coordination is positively correlated with social network centrality and that this effect is greater than previous results showing a similar connection between status-based power and linguistic coordination. We conjecture that the social value of coordination may reside in the wish to conform to the linguistic norms of a community.

1 Introduction

In communicative contexts, there is more to language use than the individual processing of representations. When two or more interlocutors take part in a conversation, they engage in a *joint* activity — a type of social interaction that requires an intricate level of interpersonal coordination. This often leads to interlocutors converging on similar patterns of language use, including phonetic production (Kim et al., 2011; Babel, 2012), lexical choice (Brennan, 1996), use of function words (Niederhoffer and Pennebaker, 2002), and of syntactic constructions (Pickering and Ferreira, 2008).

It is a matter of debate what mechanisms give rise to the observed convergences and whether different factors may simultaneously and complementarily be at play. For instance, the "collaborative" approach led by Clark (1996) considers that adaptation or entrainment is mainly motivated by the communicative need to reach mutual understanding, which leads to speakers reasoning about their common ground (Clark and Murphy, 1982; Brennan and Clark, 1996; Brennan and Hanna, 2009). In contrast, Pickering and Garrod (2004) have argued that stimulus-response priming is the key mechanism underlying alignment of representations in conversation (Branigan et al., 1995; Pickering and Garrod, 2006; Reitter and Moore, 2014). Yet, within social psychology researchers have emphasised the role of social processes and goals as triggers of linguistic "imitation" (Shepard et al., 2001; Giles, 2008; Babel, 2012).

In this paper, we contribute to this latter line of research by investigating the effects of social factors on linguistic coordination. In particular, we exploit notions of *network centrality* from Social Network Analysis (Wasserman, 1994) to study the extent to which an individual's position in a social network is connected to differences in linguistic adaptation observed within a community. We use online discussions amongst Wikipedia[1] editors as our case study, leveraging a corpus compiled by Danescu-Niculescu-Mizil et al. (2012), who found that the social status of editors (whether they have the role of administrator) is relevant to explain the patterns of linguistic coordination observed in this online community. In the present study we show that network centrality factors (which are largely implicit) also bear on linguistic coordination in this scenario, largely independently of explicit social status.

[1] https://www.wikipedia.org

Proceedings of CMCL 2015, pages 29–38,

The paper proceeds as follows: In Sections 2 and 3, we introduce key notions related to socially-driven linguistic coordination and social network analysis, respectively, and review related work in these areas. In Section 4, we put forward our working hypotheses. The experimental setup and the particular measures we use to test these hypotheses are described in Section 5. In Section 6, we present our results in detail. Finally, we conclude in Section 7 with a discussion of the implications of these results.

2 Socially-Driven Linguistic Coordination

The influence of social factors on how we linguistically communicate with each other has been studied, amongst others, by sociologists working within the framework of Conversation Analysis (Atkinson and Drew, 1979; Heritage, 2005) and by social psychologists employing more quantitative approaches such as Communication Accommodation Theory (Giles, 2008). CAT claims that linguistic adaptation is motivated by individuals' aim to be socially accepted and to negotiate the social distance that separates them from their interlocutors (increasing, maintaining, or decreasing it). Such adaptation can take place at different levels: pitch, vocabulary, gestures, etc. (Giles et al., 1991). An approach in this direction has been put forward by Pennebaker and colleagues, who focus on *style matching*, in particular the matching of function words such as pronouns, articles, and quantifiers (Chung and Pennebaker, 2007). For instance, it has been shown that function word matching in speed dating conversations predicts relationship initiation and stability (Ireland et al., 2011) and that it is indicative of relative social status between interlocutors (Niederhoffer and Pennebaker, 2002). An advantage of focusing on function words is that their choice is genuinely *stylistic*, i.e. not directly related to the topic of the conversation and thus largely domain independent.

Linguistic style matching has been exploited by Danescu-Niculescu-Mizil et al. (2012) to investigate power differences in two domains: the community of Wikipedia editors and the U.S. Supreme Court. The authors found that power differences between interlocutors bear upon the degree to which a speaker echoes the linguistic style of the addressee to whom they are responding. In the Wikipedia domain (which is the most relevant for our own study), it was observed that speakers tend to linguistically coordinate more with editors who have the role of administrator. Adminship confers a certain authority since these editors can block user accounts and protect or delete Wikipedia pages.[2] Therefore admins have a higher social status than other editors (non-admins), which endows them with *status-based power*.

We examine the same corpus of textual conversational exchanges amongst Wikipedia editors, but in addition to status-based power, we consider linguistic style coordination in relation to an individual's *position in a social network structure*. In particular, we investigate the effect that a speaker's network *centrality* has on how much other individuals coordinate with her linguistically.

3 Importance in Social Network Structure

A social network is a graph model of a community where nodes represent individuals (of some kind) and edges represent links between those individuals. Edges may be weighted to capture the strength of certain links or directed to represent asymmetrical relationships. Given a social network, one may extract information about how *important* an individual is in the community. Importance is of course a slippery notion. Which individuals are important depends on what it means to be important in a particular community and how these criteria are encoded in the network model. Network centrality is a family of measures that attempt to capture importance by assigning a numerical value to each node based on its position in the network structure. We shall consider two measures of network centrality, which will be defined in Section 5.3.

High centrality might be seen as a source of power (be it status-based or of some other kind), but this is not always so. A case in point are exchange networks: An exchange network is one where social relations involve the exchange of valued commodities, be they physical, like goods and services, or less tangible, like affection or information. In such networks, power often increases with access to non-central individuals who have less choice in partners

[2] `https://en.wikipedia.org/wiki/Wikipedia:Administrators`

for exchange. In such situations it may present a power advantage *not* to be centrally located (Cook et al., 1983). Regardless of whether importance corresponds to high or low centrality values in a particular social community, network centrality certainly does not confer any institutionalised title or explicit authority. For this reason we consider centrality as related to *implicit social power*, to be considered in parallel with status-based power.

The ease with which social network structure can be extracted from online communities has made network analysis of such communities a very active method of research in different fields concerned with social interaction at large, not necessarily with language (Chakrabarti, 2003; Guha et al., 2004; Leskovec et al., 2010). In sociolinguistics, however, the effect of network structure on language had been observed long before the prevalence of the Internet. Sociolinguists have examined the relationship between social network features and aspects of linguistic variation and change to draw conclusions on how the linguistic behaviour of individuals reflects their membership in small-scale social clusters (Milroy, 1987; Milroy and Milroy, 1997). For example, Eckert (1988) considers the effects of the social network of suburban Detroit area adolescents on their susceptibility to phonological innovations. She argues that linguistic change can be better explained by features of the social network than by unstructured demographic data and that alignment of linguistic styles is an important factor in maintaining acceptance in a rapidly developing social structure.

Thanks to the ubiquity of the Internet, it is now possible to apply social network analysis techniques to address sociolinguistic concerns to much larger amounts of linguistic data than ever before. Here we exploit this opportunity, in particular the availability of interactional data from a rich online community such as the Wikipedia editors. Although Wikipedia has been used as a testbed to study the connection between structural network properties and factors such as contentious topics (Laniado et al., 2011), quality improvement of Wikipedia articles (Kittur and Kraut, 2008) or editing activity (Crandall et al., 2008), to the best of our knowledge this is the first study that investigates the links between social network features of this community and linguistic style coordination amongst its members.

4 Hypotheses

We investigate the following three hypotheses that relate linguistic style coordination to the concept of social network centrality:

H1. *Speakers coordinate more towards individuals that occupy more central social positions.*

H2. *Individuals in more central social network positions tend to possess status-based power.*

H3. *The effect hypothesized in H1 holds independently of any effect observed in relation to H2.*

While we are primarily interested in the relationship between linguistic coordination and network centrality, we do so in a context where something is known about the status-based power born by individuals: We have access to the adminship role of editors and editors themselves are aware of the admin status of other users.[3] We expect to find that social network centrality correlates with status-based power, i.e., that individuals at the centre stage of the community are more likely to be admins (H2). With this in mind, we would like to separate the effect of status-based power on coordination from that of implicit centrality-based power (H3). Given that linguistic style coordination correlates with status-based power (Danescu-Niculescu-Mizil et al., 2012), it is not enough simply to show that it also correlates with network centrality (H1) since such a result may be wholly explained by status-based power as a confounding factor.

5 Experimental Setup

In this section we describe the corpus used in our experiments and define the measures of linguistic coordination and network centrality that we compute from the data.

5.1 Data

The Wikipedia Talk Page Conversations Corpus consists of a collection of exchanges from Wikipedia editors' *user talk pages*. A talk page, as opposed to a Wikipedia *article*, is a page for discussion between

[3]There is a symbol identifying admins as such on their Wikipedia user page, although it is worth noting that no such identifying marks are visible where discussions take place.

editors that is not part of the content of Wikipedia. User talk pages, which are not associated with a particular article, tend to feature more community-oriented discussions.[4]

The corpus contains information on 26,397 users, including whether or not the editor is a Wikipedia administrator (an *admin*). There are 1,825 admins. Each utterance (or *post*) is annotated with metadata including the username of the editor who made the post and which previous contribution it is a reply to (if any). Of 391,294 total posts in the corpus, we consider a subset of 342,800 that were made by users whose admin status is known (i.e., by one of the 26,397 for whom we have metadata). The corpus was collected in August 2011 and made available by Danescu-Niculescu-Mizil et al. (2012).[5]

We derived a weighted network structure from the corpus as follows: A node was created for each individual. Undirected, weighted edges were formed between editors based on the number of direct replies between them. An edge with weight w between user a and user b indicates that w is the total number of times user a replied to a post of user b or *visa versa*. The edges in this model are intended to represent the degree to which two users *know* each other (as members of the Wikipedia editors' community). The talk page is the locus of an editor's involvement in Wikipedia as a community. The rationale for our edge definition is that a's reply to b's contribution is directed at b *as a member* of the community. The more that a and b reply to one another, the better connected they are in the network.

The resulting network was pruned to its largest connected component such that there is a path between every pair of nodes. Pruning eliminated 575 users from 556 different disconnected components (mostly singletons). The final network consists of 25,822 nodes and 103,992 edges with an average weight of 3.3.

5.2 Linguistic Coordination Measures

We want to measure how much participants align their language with that of the interlocutors to whom they are immediately replying. Following Danescu-Niculescu-Mizil et al. (2012), we use the presence of a word in a particular category of *function words* as linguistic style markers. We consider the same eight categories of functional markers as these authors: quantifiers, personal pronouns, impersonal pronouns, articles, auxiliary verbs, conjunctions, prepositions, and adverbs. However, while Danescu-Niculeascu-Mizil and colleagues use the markers provided by the commercial text analysis software LIWC (Pennebaker et al., 2007),[6] we compiled our own list of markers for each of these eight categories using freely available frequency lists of part-of-speech classes from the British National Corpus (Burnard, 2000).[7] We took the most common words for each relevant POS (manually filtering out any content words) to match the length of the LIWC category lists reported in the software documentation.[8]

Linguistic style coordination quantifies the degree to which an agent b immediately echoes the linguistic style of agent a. We use the linguistic style coordination measure $C^m(b, a)$ defined by Danescu-Niculeascu-Mizil, et al. (2012), where the coordination of b (the *speaker*) towards a (the *target*) with respect to a marker m encodes how much a's use of m increases the probability that b will use that marker in her reply to a, relative to the overall frequency of m in b's replies to a:[9]

$$C^m(b, a) = P(\mathcal{E}^m_{u_b} \mid \mathcal{E}^m_{u_a}) - P(\mathcal{E}^m_{u_b})$$

where $\mathcal{E}^m_u$ indicates that utterance u exhibits a marker m and (u_a, u_b) belongs to the set of pairs of utterances made by b in response to a. If none of the utterances of a that b responds to exhibit m, then $C^m(b, a)$ is undefined.

We introduce a variant of this measure that considers the coordination of a group of speakers B towards an individual a by making the same calculation across all utterance pairs (u_a, u_B) where some member of B is replying to individual a. When B

[4] http://en.wikipedia.org/wiki/Wikipedia:Talk_page_guidelines

[5] http://www.cs.cornell.edu/~cristian/Echoes_of_power.html

[6] http://www.liwc.net

[7] http://ucrel.lancs.ac.uk/bncfreq/flists.html

[8] The relevant LIWC documentation can be found at http://www.liwc.net/descriptiontable1.php. Our lists of markers are freely available upon request.

[9] This ensures that $C^m(b, a)$ captures the influence of a's use of marker m on b's immediate reply. It may be that b uses m more *in general* when speaking to a, but such an effect would have no bearing on $C^m(b, a)$.

is the set of all members of a social network who have addressed a, we refer to $C^m(B, a)$ as a's *coordination received*. This is the main measure we will employ in the analyses reported in Section 6.

It is sometimes desirable to have a single score that combines a's coordination received across all markers. This is made complicated by the fact that coordination may be undefined for one or more markers. Since we generally consider coordination received by a in the context of a's membership in some group A (e.g., admins), there are several different aggregation schemes available. Again, we follow Danescu-Niculeascu-Mizil et al. (2012) in the naming and definition of these schemes, but apply them to *coordination received*.

Aggregate 1 Take a simple average across markers, but only for those users a in A for whom $C^m(B, a)$ is defined for all markers. Otherwise the aggregate is undefined for a.

Aggregate 2 Wherever $C^m(B, a)$ is undefined, substitute with the average of $C^m(B, a')$ across those a' in A for whom it is defined.

Aggregate 3 Whenever $C^m(B, a)$ is undefined, substitute with the average of $C^{m'}(B, a)$ across those m' for which it is defined.

When taking an average aggregate coordination received over a group of users A, aggregate 1 takes into account only those users for whom all measures are defined. Aggregates 2 and 3 take into account all users for whom at least one measure is defined, but exhibit slightly different smoothing assumptions. Aggregate 2 assumes that people in B would have behaved towards a with regard to m as they did towards the rest of A, whereas aggregate 3 assumes that members of B would have behaved towards a with regard to m as they did with regard to the other markers.

5.3 Network Centrality Measures

As mentioned in Section 3, a network centrality measure assigns a numerical value to each individual in the network based on features of their position in the graph. This value is intended to represent the importance of that individual in the social network. What kind of importance it captures depends on exactly how centrality is calculated. Here we consider two well-known measures of network centrality.

Eigenvector centrality (Bonacich, 1987) tries to capture the notion that your importance in a network depends on the importance of your closest contacts. Let $M(n)$ be the *neighborhood* of n; that is, the nodes in N that share an edge with n. Then the Eigenvector centrality of n^* is defined by

$$\mathrm{EC}(n^*) = \frac{1}{\lambda} \sum_{n \in M(n^*)} \mathrm{EC}(n)$$

where λ is a constant, the *eigenvalue*. There may be multiple values of λ for which the Eigenvector centrality is defined, but taking the largest value provides a consistent measure across the network.

Betweenness centrality (Freeman, 1977) measures how much a node contributes to the overall connectivity of the network. Nodes who lie on more *shortest paths* between pairs of other nodes have higher Betweenness centrality. Specifically it looks at all of the shortest paths between each pair of nodes, and counts how many of them contain the node in question. Letting $\mathrm{Path}(m, n)$ stand for the set of shortest paths between m and n, the Betweenness centrality of n^* is defined by:

$$\mathrm{BC}(n^*) = \sum_{n \neq m \in N} \frac{|\{\sigma \in \mathrm{Path}(m, n) | n^* \in \sigma\}|}{|\mathrm{Path}(m, n)|}$$

Both Eigenvector and Betweenness centrality measures have generalizations for weighted networks which we use here. For Betweenness, path length is calculated using the inverse weight of edges (so that paths along edges with higher weights are considered shorter). For Eigenvector centrality, the notion of "neighbour" is adjusted so that adjacent nodes connected with a higher weight count for more. We use the implementation of these algorithms available in the Python library NetworkX (Hagberg et al., 2008).[10]

6 Analyses and Results

To investigate our hypotheses regarding the impact of social network position on linguistic coordination, we computed scores for all the measures in-

[10] `https://networkx.github.io`

	Agg. 3	Eigenvector	Betweenness	Users
admins	1.85 (6.44)	1.01 (15.9)	1.66 (9.44)	1825
non-admins	0.48 (6.85)	0.16 (4.72)	0.14 (2.67)	23,997
Total	0.60 (6.83)	0.22 (6.22)	0.25 (3.62)	25,822

Table 1: Descriptive statistics of the computed measures: Averages (and standard deviations) for Coordination received according to Aggregate 3 (scaled by 100), Eigenvector and Betweenness centrality (scaled by 1000) for admin and non-admin users.

troduced in the previous section (coordination received, Eigenvector and Betweenness centrality) for each individual in the social network. Table 1 provides some basic descriptive statistics.

6.1 Coordination and Status-Based Power

We start by replicating the relevant result by Danescu-Niculescu-Mizil et al. (2012), according to which Wikipedia editors coordinate more towards admins than non-admins. We compare the average linguistic coordination received by each of these two social groups for each functional marker as well as for each of the aggregate measures. The results are shown in Figure 1. As can be seen, in all cases individuals coordinate significantly more towards admin addressees than towards non-admins (independent Welch two sample t-test, $p < 0.001$). We are thus able to reproduce this basic result despite the fact that we use a self-compiled list of functional markers instead of the full power of the LIWC tool (Pennebaker et al., 2007). The results we obtain are in fact stronger, since we observe high levels of significance for all aggregate measures and markers while Danescu-Nicolescu-Mizil and colleagues obtained significant results only for the aggregate measures and for conjunctions, indefinite pronouns, adverbs and articles. We point out however that regardless of the high significance values across the board, the size of the effect is larger for the aggregate measures (average Cohen's $d = 0.2$) than for any of the individual markers (for which the effect size is in fact very small: on average $d < 0.15$).[11]

6.2 Coordination and Centrality

We now turn to investigate each of the hypotheses formulated in Section 4. Our data provide evidence

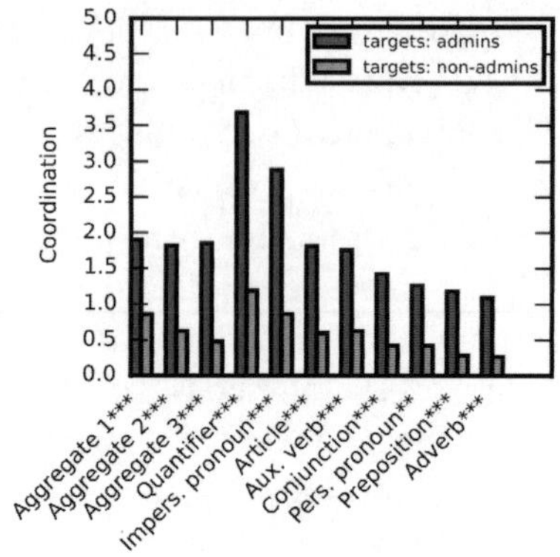

Figure 1: Linguistic style coordination towards admins/non-admins. Note on all figures: Coordination scores are reported as percentages for clarity (i.e., multiplied by 100). Measures are marked for significance by independent t-test as follows: $* = p < 0.05$, $** = p < 0.01$, $*** = p < 0.001$.

in support of H1 (*speakers coordinate more towards individuals that occupy more central social positions*). As shown in Table 2, we find significant (albeit weak) positive correlations in all cases between the level of coordination received by an individual a ($C^m(B, a)$) and a's position in the social network, as quantified by Eigenvector and Betweenness centrality scores.[12] Betweenness centrality correlates slightly better with coordination received.

	Agg. 1	Agg. 2	Agg. 3
Eigenvector	0.1911	0.1175	0.1878
Betweenness	0.2028	0.1491	0.2113

Table 2: Spearman's rank correlation ρ between network centrality measures and linguistic coordination received ($p < 0.001$ for all values).

We consider an individual *highly central* with respect to some centrality measure if this individual's centrality score is higher than one standard deviation above the mean score. Given the large amount of variation in our dataset (see Table 1), this is a very selective criterion: Out of 25,822 editors, only 119 ($\sim$0.5%) are highly Eigenvector-central and 239 ($\sim$0.9%) are highly Betweenness-central. We observe that speakers coordinate more with individu-

[11] Danescu-Niculescu-Mizil et al. (2012) do not report effect size and hence a more detailed comparison is not possible.

[12] This is also the case for the individual markers, which are not shown in Table 2 for conciseness.

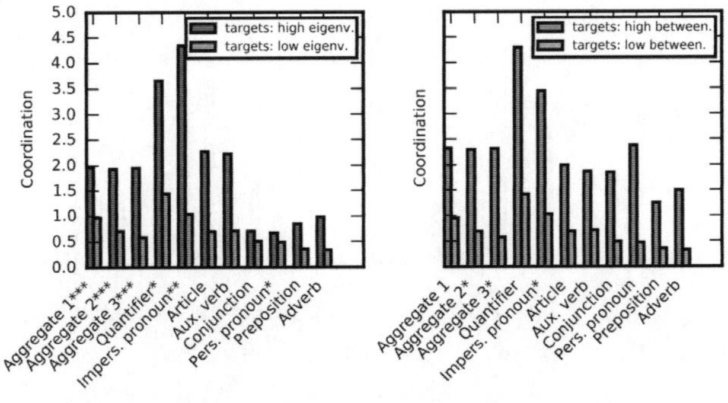

Figure 2: Linguistic style coordination towards users with high/low Eigenvector and Betweenness centrality.

als that are highly central, significantly so for most of the aggregate measures, pronouns and quantifiers (independent Welch two sample t-test; see Figure 2). The average effect size for the aggregate measures is $d = 0.32$ for Eigenvector centrality and $d = 0.35$ for Betweenness centrality.

Regarding H2 (*individuals in more central social network positions tend to possess status-based power*), in our dataset only 29% of editors who are highly Eigenvector-central are also admins. The percentage goes up to 53% in the case of highly Betweenness-central editors. Editors with admin status make up around 45% of those individuals who are highly central according to at least one measure (319 editors) and around 49% of those who are highly central according to both measures (39 editors). To further investigate the connection between status-based power as represented by adminship and network centrality, we examined the mean centrality scores of admin versus non-admin editors. We find that on average admins are more centrally positioned in the network than non-admins. An independent Welch t-test confirms that this is significant for both Eigenvector centrality ($p < 0.5$, Cohen's $d = 0.07$) and Betweenness centrality ($p < 0.001$, Cohen's $d = 0.22$), although the effect is practically nonexistent for the former centrality measure. Thus, H2 is only relatively supported, with Betweenness centrality exhibiting a closer connection with adminship than Eigenvector centrality.

Finally, to assess H3 (*the effect hypothesized in H1 holds independently of any effect observed in relation to H2*), we compared the average coordination received scores for admins and non-admins within each class of highly central users. Our aim was to check whether users coordinate more towards editors who are both administrators and highly central in the social network. As shown in Figure 3 (left), no effects of adminship were found (for all markers and aggregate measures, $p > 0.05$ in an independent Welch t-test), which provides evidence supporting the hypothesis. Analogous calculations were made for users who are not highly central (Figure 3, right). Amongst these, significant differences were found (albeit with small effect sizes: $0.16 < d < 0.2$ across the board for both centrality measures), with admins receiving more linguistic coordination for all markers and aggregate measures.[13]

7 Discussion and Conclusions

In this paper we have put forward the hypothesis that speakers coordinate more with targets who occupy a more central position in the social context in which the communication takes place. We have provided evidence for this claim by measuring linguistic style coordination in the Wikipedia talk pages corpus.

We confirmed the result by Danescu-Niculescu-Mizil et al. (2012) that correlates coordination with explicit status-based power represented by adminship, and went on to show that there is a further positive relationship between how much linguistic style coordination an editor receives and her network centrality. Furthermore, while editors coordinate more with admins in general, we found that adminship has no significant effect on how much coordination *highly central* editors receive. We may conclude that in certain situations, considerations of network centrality trump explicit status-based power in determining how much a speaker immediately aligns with the person to whom she is responding.

This conclusion provides evidence for the claim of Communication Accommodation Theory according to which linguistic adaptation is motivated by the desire for social acceptance (Giles, 2008). Exactly how aligning with highly central members of

[13] We chose this analysis over a regression analysis because the data violates the normality assumption and is affected by very severe heteroscedasticity, i.e., the variance in the error is not constant, with very large residuals when the centrality measures are low and much smaller ones as they increase.

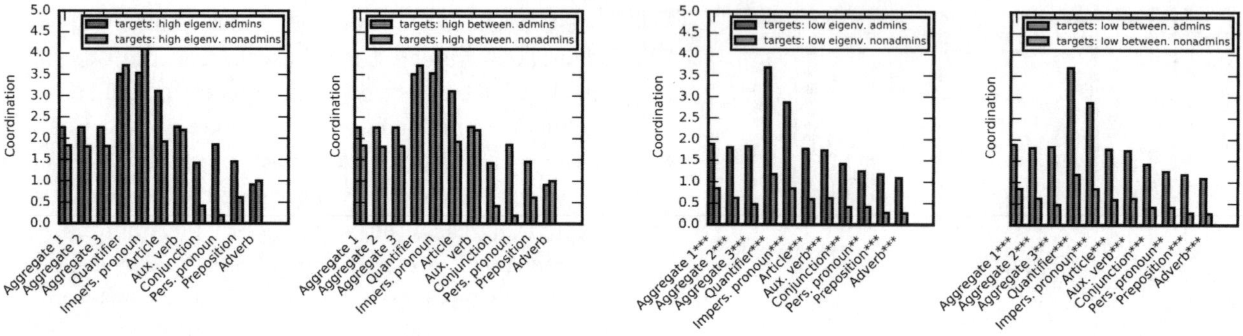

Figure 3: Linguistic style coordination towards admins/non-admins among users with high (left) and low (right) Eigenvector/Betweenness centrality.

the community achieves this goal is open to some interpretation, though it is likely that there is more than one mechanism at play. We consider two possibilities.

First, aligning with highly central community members can be seen as an instance of aligning to power, since network centrality (especially Eigenvector centrality) is often used as a proxy for implicit social power. Aligning with highly central members helps to achieve social acceptance since those with implicit social power have more power to grant it. This interpretation is supported by our results: Just as coordination more closely follows network centrality than it does adminship, it is natural to assume that the power to confer social acceptance more closely follows implicit social power than it does any official title.

The second possible interpretation has more expressly linguistic motivations. It has been observed that those in central social positions make more utterances characteristic of the group they are central to (Eckert, 1988; Kooti et al., 2012). Since learning the linguistic practices of a community is important to social acceptance, it is beneficial to coordinate with highly central members of the community as a way of picking up those linguistic practices. In other words, coordination towards a highly central individual may have a social goal that does not have anything to do with that individual in particular, but rather with adapting to the linguistic norms of the community at large.

Although Eigenvector centrality is most closely associated with implicit power (Bonacich, 1987), we found that in the Wikipedia corpus it is actually Betweenness centrality that correlates somewhat more strongly with coordination. This may have something to say about the relationship between the two mechanisms mentioned above. While it may still be true that people align to power for the immediate social benefit, the greater effect of Betweenness centrality suggests that the social benefit of coordination may be mediated by something more than the power of the individual who is being responded to. One possible explanation is that community members who are more vital to the connectivity of the social network (i.e., those with high Betweenness centrality) tend to conform better with the linguistic norms of the community as a whole (rather than, for example, to the norms of some clique or subgroup). Assuming that some of the social motivations for alignment are expressly linguistic, this would explain why Betweenness centrality correlates better with coordination received than the centrality measure more typically associated with social power. More research is needed to determine whether (a) community members with high Betweenness centrality better represent the linguistic norms of the community and (b) immediate linguistic coordination is the mechanism by which those norms are propagated.

The results of this paper are suggestive in both those regards, while providing good evidence that, at the very least, network centrality is a more important factor in linguistic coordination than is formal status-based power.

References

John Maxwell Atkinson and Paul Drew. 1979. *Order in court: The organisation of verbal interaction in judicial settings.* Macmillan London.

Molly Babel. 2012. Evidence for phonetic and social selectivity in spontaneous phonetic imitation. *Journal of Phonetics*, 40(1):177–189.

Phillip Bonacich. 1987. Power and centrality: A family of measures. *American journal of sociology*, pages 1170–1182.

Holly P. Branigan, Martin J. Pickering, Simon P. Liversedge, Andrew J. Stewart, and Thomas P. Urbach. 1995. Syntactic priming: Investigating the mental representation of language. *Journal of Psycholinguistic Research*, 24(6):489–506.

Susan E. Brennan and Herbert H. Clark. 1996. Conceptual Pacts and Lexical Choice in Conversation. *Journal of Experimental Psychology*, 22(6):1482–1493.

Susan E. Brennan and Joy E. Hanna. 2009. Partner-specific adaptation in dialog. *Topics in Cognitive Science*, 1(2):274–291.

Susan E. Brennan. 1996. Lexical entrainment in spontaneous dialog. In *Proc. of the International Symposium on Spoken Dialogue*, pages 41–44.

Lou Burnard. 2000. *Reference Guide for the British National Corpus (World Edition).* Oxford University Computing Services.

Soumen Chakrabarti. 2003. *Mining the Web: Discovering knowledge from hypertext data.* Morgan Kaufmann.

Cindy Chung and James W. Pennebaker. 2007. The psychological functions of function words. *Social Communication*, pages 343–359.

Herbert H. Clark and Gregory L. Murphy. 1982. Audience design in meaning and reference. *Advances in psychology*, 9:287–299.

Herbert H. Clark. 1996. *Using language.* CUP.

Karen S. Cook, Richard M. Emerson, Mary R. Gillmore, and Toshio Yamagishi. 1983. The distribution of power in exchange networks: Theory and experimental results. *American journal of sociology*, pages 275–305.

David Crandall, Dan Cosley, Daniel Huttenlocher, Jon Kleinberg, and Siddharth Suri. 2008. Feedback effects between similarity and social influence in online communities. In *Proceedings of the 14th ACM SIGKDD international conference on Knowledge discovery and data mining*, pages 160–168.

Cristian Danescu-Niculescu-Mizil, Lillian Lee, Bo Pang, and Jon Kleinberg. 2012. Echoes of power: Language effects and power differences in social interaction. In *Proceedings of the 21st international conference on World Wide Web*, pages 699–708. ACM.

Penelope Eckert. 1988. Adolescent social structure and the spead of linguistic change. *Language in Society*, 17(2):183–207.

Linton C. Freeman. 1977. A set of measures of centrality based on betweenness. *Sociometry*, pages 35–41.

Howard Giles, Justine Coupland, and Nikolas Coupland. 1991. Accommodation theory: Communication, context, and consequence. *Contexts of accommodation: Developments in applied sociolinguistics*, 1.

Howard Giles. 2008. Communication accommodation theory. In Leslie A. Baxter and Dawn O. Braithewaite, editors, *Engaging theories in interpersonal communication: Multiple perspectives*, pages 161–173. Sage Publications, Inc.

Ramanthan Guha, Ravi Kumar, Prabhakar Raghavan, and Andrew Tomkins. 2004. Propagation of trust and distrust. In *Proceedings of the 13th international conference on World Wide Web*, pages 403–412.

Aric A. Hagberg, Daniel A. Schult, and Pieter J. Swart. 2008. Exploring network structure, dynamics, and function using NetworkX. In *Proceedings of the 7th Python in Science Conference (SciPy2008)*, pages 11–15, Pasadena, CA USA, August.

John Heritage. 2005. Conversation analysis and institutional talk. In *Handbook of language and social interaction*, pages 103–147. Erlbaum.

Molly E. Ireland, Richard B. Slatcher, Paul W. Eastwick, Lauren E. Scissors, Eli J. Finkel, and James W. Pennebaker. 2011. Language style matching predicts relationship initiation and stability. *Psychological Science*, 22(1):39–44.

Midam Kim, William S. Horton, and Ann R. Bradlow. 2011. Phonetic convergence in spontaneous conversations as a function of interlocutor language distance. *Laboratory Phonology*, 2(1):125–156.

Aniket Kittur and Robert E. Kraut. 2008. Harnessing the wisdom of crowds in wikipedia: quality through coordination. In *Proceedings of the 2008 ACM conference on Computer supported cooperative work*, pages 37–46.

Farshad Kooti, Haeryun Yang, Meeyoung Cha, Krishna P. Gummadi, and Winter A Mason. 2012. The emergence of conventions in online social networks. In *ICWSM.*

David Laniado, Riccardo Tasso, Yana Volkovich, and Andreas Kaltenbrunner. 2011. When the Wikipedians talk: Network and tree structure of Wikipedia discussion pages. In *ICWSM*.

Jure Leskovec, Daniel Huttenlocher, and Jon Kleinberg. 2010. Predicting positive and negative links in online social networks. In *Proceedings of the 19th international conference on World Wide Web*, pages 641–650.

James Milroy and Lesley Milroy. 1997. Network structure and linguistic change. In Nikolas Coupland and Adam Jaworski, editors, *Sociolinguistics: a reader*. St. Martin's Press.

Lesley Milroy. 1987. *Language and Social Networks*. Oxford: Blackwell, 2nd edition.

Kate G Niederhoffer and James W Pennebaker. 2002. Linguistic style matching in social interaction. *Journal of Language and Social Psychology*, 21(4):337–360.

James W. Pennebaker, Martha E. Francis, and Roger J. Booth. 2007. Linguistic Inquiry and Word Count (LIWC): A computerized text analysis program. Technical report, LIWC.net, Austin, Texas.

Martin J. Pickering and Victor S. Ferreira. 2008. Structural priming: a critical review. *Psychological Bulletin*, 134(3):427–459.

Martin J. Pickering and Simon Garrod. 2004. Toward a mechanistic psychology of dialogue. *Behavioral and Brain Sciences*, 27(02):169–190.

Martin J. Pickering and Simon Garrod. 2006. Alignment as the basis for successful communication. *Research on Language and Computation*, 4(2-3):203–228.

David Reitter and Johanna D. Moore. 2014. Alignment and task success in spoken dialogue. *Journal of Memory and Language*, 76:29–46.

Carolyn A. Shepard, Howard Giles, and Beth A. Le Poire. 2001. Communication accommodation theory. In W. P. Robinson and H. Giles, editors, *The new Handbook of Language and Social Psychology*, pages 33–56. John Wiley & Sons Ltd.

Stanley Wasserman. 1994. *Social network analysis: Methods and applications*, volume 8. Cambridge University Press.

Fusion of Compositional Network-based and Lexical Function Distributional Semantic Models

Spiros Georgiladakis
School of ECE
National Technical University of Athens
Athens, Greece
sgeorgil@central.ntua.gr

Elias Iosif
School of ECE
National Technical University of Athens
"Athena" Research Center
Athens, Greece
iosife@central.ntua.gr

Alexandros Potamianos
School of ECE
National Technical University of Athens
"Athena" Research Center
Athens, Greece
potam@central.ntua.gr

Abstract

Distributional Semantic Models (DSMs) have been successful at modeling the meaning of individual words, with interest recently shifting to compositional structures, i.e., phrases and sentences. Network-based DSMs represent and handle semantics via operators applied on word neighborhoods, i.e., semantic graphs containing a target's most similar words. We extend network-based DSMs to address compositionality using an activation model (motivated by psycholinguistics) that operates on the fused neighborhoods of variable size activation. The proposed method is evaluated against and combined with the lexical function method proposed by (Baroni and Zamparelli, 2010). We show that, by fusing a network-based with a lexical function model, performance gains can be achieved.

1 Introduction

Vector Space Models (VSMs) have proven their efficiency at representing word semantics, which are vital components for numerous natural language applications, such as paraphrasing and textual entailment (Androutsopoulos and Malakasiotis, 2010), affective text analysis (Malandrakis et al., 2013), etc. VSMs constitute the most-widely used implementation of Distributional Semantic Models (DSMs) (Baroni and Lenci, 2010). A fundamental task addressed in the framework of DSMs is the computation of semantic similarity between words, adopting the distributional hypothesis of meaning, i.e., *"similarity of context implies similarity of meaning"* (Harris, 1954). DSMs have been successful when applied to the representation of word lexical semantics, enabling the computation of word semantic similarity (Turney and Pantel, 2010). However, the application of DSMs for representing the semantics of more complex structures, e.g., phrases or sentences, is not trivial since the meaning of such structures is the result of various compositional phenomena (Pelletier, 1994) that are inherent properties of natural language creativity. The key idea behind current approaches in semantic composition (using DSMs) is the combination of word vectors using simple functions, e.g., vector addition or multiplication (Mitchell and Lapata, 2008; Mitchell and Lapata, 2010), or other transformational functions. Regardless of the used function, the resulting representations adhere to the paradigm of VSMs, while the cosine between the (composed) vectors is used for estimating similarity. Such efforts proved to be effective when computing the similarity between two-word phrases, however, their limitations were revealed for the case of longer structures (Polajnar et al., 2014), where the composition of meaning becomes more complex. Bengio and Mikolov (2003; 2013) proposed an approach based on deep learning for building language models that address the prob-

Proceedings of CMCL 2015, pages 39–47,
Denver, Colorado, June 4, 2015. ©2015 Association for Computational Linguistics

lem of language creativity. The models appear to constantly gain support in comparison with the traditional DSMs. A preliminary comparative analysis of them is provided in (Baroni et al., 2014b) with respect to a number of tasks related to lexical semantics.

In this work, we extend a recent network-based implementation of DSMs (Iosif and Potamianos, 2015) in order to represent the semantics of compositional structures. The used framework consists of activation models motivated by semantic priming (McNamara, 2005). For each structure, an activation area (i.e, semantic neighborhood) is computed which is regarded as a sub-space within the network. The novelty of the present work is two-fold. First, we propose various approaches for the creation of activation areas for compositional structures, within a framework alternative to VSMs. Second, we investigate the fusion of the proposed network-based model with VSM-based transformational approaches from the literature. In addition, we investigate the role of words as operators on the meaning of the structures they occur in by measuring their transformative degree.

The remainder of this paper is organized as follows: in Section 2 we describe work related to DSMs. In Section 3 we describe the work on which we based the proposed models. We present the proposed models in Section 4. The lexical function model is described in Section 5, and a fusion model integrating the former with network-based models is proposed. We describe the experimental procedure that we followed and evaluate the proposed models in Section 6. We elaborate on the effects of modifiers in compositional structures in Section 7, concluding in Section 8.

2 Related Work

Word-level DSMs can be categorized into unstructured, that employ a bag-of-words model, and structured, that employ syntactic relationships between words (Grefenstette, 1994; Baroni and Lenci, 2010). DSMs are typically constructed from co-occurrence statistics of word tuples. An unstructured approach for the construction of network-based DSMs was proposed in (Iosif and Potamianos, 2015), where nodes represent words, and edges are formulated according to the semantic similarity of the connected nodes. For each node, the notion of semantic neighborhood (i.e., the most semantically similar words) is utilized for estimating an improved similarity between the nodes.

Moving beyond the word-level, Turney (2012) proposed a "dual-space" model that combines relational and compositional methods for representing phrasal semantics. This approach utilized two complementary models in an attempt to address a series of phenomena that apply to compositional semantics, namely, "linguistic creativity", "order sensitivity", "adaptive capacity", and "information scalability"[1]. Three types of phrases were investigated: noun-noun (NN), adjective-noun (AN), and verb-object (VO). In (Baroni and Zamparelli, 2010), particular focus was given to the AN type, where adjectives were represented as matrices acting as functions to the vectorial representation of head nouns. Recent research efforts have been expanded to longer text segments such as sentences (Agirre et al., 2012; Agirre et al., 2013; Polajnar et al., 2014). In (Socher et al., 2012), based on the functional space proposed in (Baroni and Zamparelli, 2010), phrase constituents were treated as both a continuous vector and a parameter matrix, where the representation of sentence semantics was constructed via a recursive bottom-up procedure.

3 Baseline Network-based Model

In this section, we generalize the ideas regarding network-based DSMs presented in (Iosif and Potamianos, 2015), for the case of more complex structures. The network consists of two layers: 1) *activation*, and 2) *similarity* layer. Given a lexical unit, the first layer represents an activation area that includes a set of lexical units that are semantically related with it. The notion of "lexical unit" refers to any semantically coherent lexical structure, spanning from words (unigrams) up to word sequences (n-grams). The second layer is used for the computation of semantic similarity between two lexical units, based on their respective activation layers. The network can be defined as a graph $Q = (V, E)$ whose set of vertices V includes the lexical units un-

[1]These phenomena are defined and discussed in (Turney, 2012)

der investigation and whose set of edges E contains links between the vertices. The links between the lexical units in the network are weighted according to their pairwise semantic similarity.

3.1 Layer 1: Activation Model

The activation layer of a lexical unit, ξ, can be regarded as a sub-graph of Q, Q_ξ, also referred to as the semantic neighborhood of ξ. Its vertices (neighbors of ξ) are determined according to their semantic similarity with ξ. Given a set of lexical units, the most similar to ξ are selected as neighbors. The activation layer is motivated by the phenomenon of semantic priming (McNamara, 2005), especially for highly coherent lexical units, such as unigrams and bigrams. In the framework of DSMs, activation layers were computed for the case of unigrams in (Iosif and Potamianos, 2015), and were extended to short phrases (bigrams) in (Iosif, 2013). Consider a phrase, $i = (i_1\ i_2)$, where i_1 and i_2 denote its first and second constituent. Assuming that the N_{i_1} and N_{i_2} sets represent neighborhoods of i_1 and i_2, respectively, the neighborhood of i, N_i, was computed by taking the intersection of N_{i_1} and N_{i_2}.

3.2 Layer 2: Semantic Model

Two similarity metrics are defined for computing the similarity between two lexical units, i and j. The metrics are defined on top of their respective activation models, N_i and N_j, computed in the previous layer. This approach relies on two assumptions, namely, maximum sense and attributional similarity, for unigrams. In this work, we extend these metrics to bigrams (see Fig. 1 and Fig. 2) in order to compute the semantic similarity between two phrases, $i = (i_1\ i_2)$ and $j = (j_1\ j_2)$, exploiting their respective activation layers N_i and N_j.

Maximum Neighborhood Similarity. The key idea of this metric, M, is the computation of similarities between the constituents of phrase i (i_1 and i_2) and the members of N_j. The same is done for j_1 and j_2 and the members of N_i. The similarity between i and j (e.g., "assistant manager" and "board member" in Fig. 1) is computed by taking the maximum of the aforementioned similarities (0.50 in Fig. 1). The underlying hypothesis is that the neighborhoods encode senses that are shared between the constituents. The selection of the maxi-

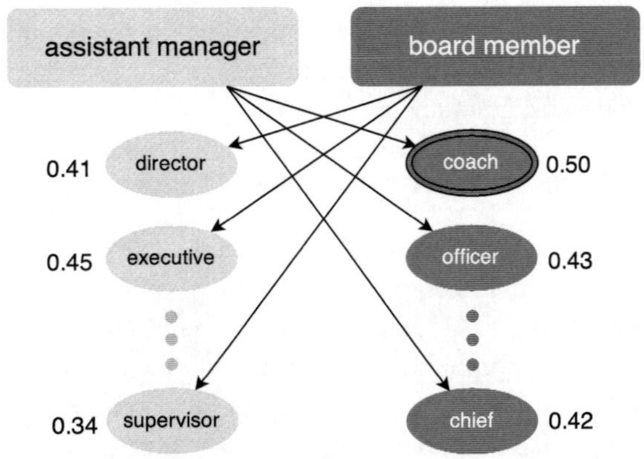

Figure 1: Maximum neighborhood similarity metric (M): bigram usecase.

mum score suggests that the similarity between i and j can be approximated by considering their closest senses (Iosif and Potamianos, 2015).

Attributional Neighborhood Similarity. In this metric, R, similarities between i_1 and i_2 and the members of N_j are computed and stored into a vector. This is also done for j_1 and j_2 and the members of N_j. The correlation coefficient between the two vectors (e.g., the two right-most vectors in Fig. 2) is computed. The process is repeated, using N_i in the place of N_j, which results into another correlation coefficient. The similarity between i and j

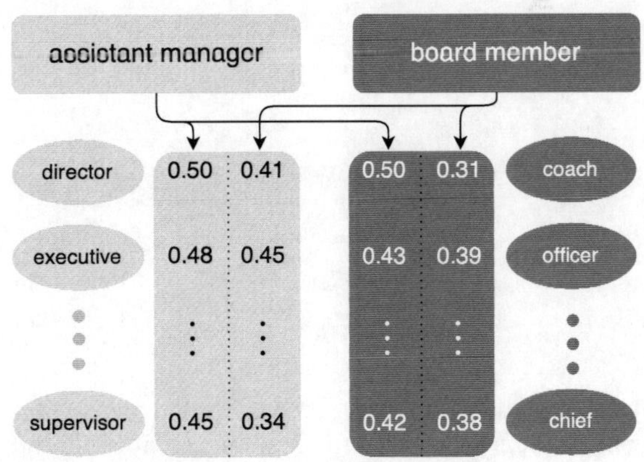

Figure 2: Attributional neighborhood similarity metric (R): bigram usecase.

is estimated by selecting the maximum correlation coefficient. The underlying motivation is attributional similarity, i.e., the hypothesis that the neighborhoods encode semantic or affective features. Semantically similar phrases are expected to exhibit correlated similarities with respect to such features (Iosif and Potamianos, 2015).

4 Extended Network-based Model

The major limitation of the model presented in Section 3 is that the neighborhoods of phrase constituents (e.g., N_{i_1} and N_{i_2}) are of fixed size. This allows the computation of an empty neighborhood for the phrase (e.g., N_i), when there is no overlap between the neighborhoods of its constituents.

In this section, we propose an extension of the aforementioned model by relaxing the hard constraint regarding the fixed size of neighborhoods. The intuition behind this idea is that the activation areas are not of the same size for all words. For example, a semantically abstract word, such as "democracy", is expected to have a larger neighborhood compared to semantically concrete words, e.g., "computer". Given a phrase, e.g., $i = (i_1\ i_2)$, in order to compute the activation N_i, we gradually extend the activation areas (i.e., sizes) of N_{i_1} and N_{i_2} until a minimum size θ for N_i is reached.

4.1 Layer 1: Activation Model

We propose three different schemes for the computation of neighborhoods. An example of those

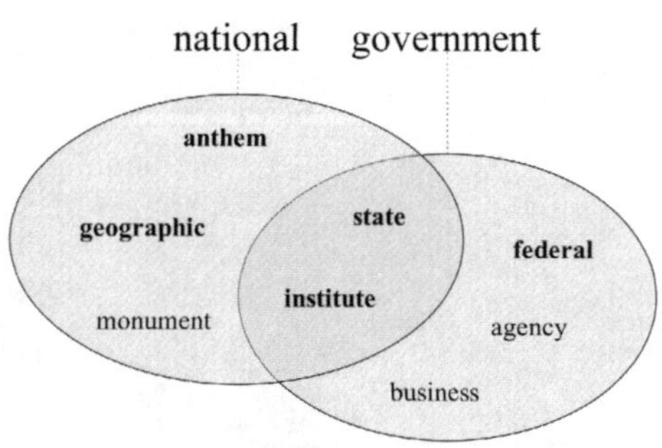

Figure 3: Activation model schemes for the phrase "national government": intersection-based, union-based, and selection of most similar neighbors (words in bold).

schemes is depicted in Fig. 3.

Scheme 1. The phrase neighborhood is computed by taking the intersection of the constituent neighborhoods, i.e., $N_i = N_{i_1} \cap N_{i_2}$. This adheres to findings from the literature of psycholinguistics suggesting that the phrase activation (and, thus, the respective meaning) should be more specific than those of its constituents (Osherson and Smith, 1981).

Scheme 2. The union of neighborhoods is used, i.e., $N_i = N_{i_1} \cup N_{i_2}$. This is motivated by the idea that, in some cases, a phrase may be associated with a larger activation area, compared to those of its constituents.

Scheme 3. The members of the phrase neighborhood are selected based on their average semantic similarity with respect to the phrase constituents. Let N_i be $\{n_1, ..., n_m, ..., n_\theta\}$, where $n_m \in \{N_{i_1} \cup N_{i_2}\}$. The N_i set can be regarded as a list, which is ranked according to $\frac{1}{2}(S(n_m, i_1)+S(n_m, i_2))$, where $S(.)$ stands for a metric of semantic similarity. This scheme is motivated by the idea that different areas of N_{i_1} and N_{i_2} may be activated given the context of words i_1 and i_2, respectively. The scheme also addresses the issue of scalability: the phrase neighborhood has the same size as the constituents' neighborhoods, enabling the recursive application of the model over longer structures.

4.2 Layer 2: Semantic Model

An extension of the M metric (described in Section 3) is proposed, along with two more metrics for computing the semantic similarity between lexical units utilizing their respective neighborhoods. The metrics are defined with respect to two lexical units, i and j, which are represented by their neighborhoods, N_i and N_j, respectively.

Average of top-k similarities (M_k). This metric extends the M metric (see Section 3) by considering the top k similarity scores instead of the maximum score. Similarity between i and j, $M_k(i, j)$, is computed by taking the arithmetic mean of the k scores.

Average of top-k pairwise similarities (P_k). Let C be a ranked list including the pairwise similarities computed between the members of N_i and N_j:

$$C = \{ \underset{\substack{x \in N_i \\ y \in N_j}}{S}(x, y) \}, \quad (1)$$

where $S(.)$ stands for a metric of semantic similarity. The similarity between i and j is computed as:

$$P_k(i, j) = \frac{1}{k} \sum_{l=1}^{k} c_l, \quad (2)$$

where c_l is the l–th member of C.

Hausdorff-based similarity (H). This metric is

motivated by the Hausdorff distance (Hung and Yang, 2004). Let $h(N_i, N_j)$ be defined as

$$h(N_i, N_j) = \min_{x \in N_i} \{\max_{y \in N_j} \{S(x, y)\}\}, \quad (3)$$

where $S(.)$ is a semantic similarity metric. The similarity between i and j is computed as:

$$H(i, j) = \max\{h(N_i, N_j), h(N_j, N_i)\} \quad (4)$$

5 Fusion of Lexical Function with Network-based Models

The representation of phrase semantics requires the consideration of the consituents' functional influence on the composed meaning. For example, when considering an adjective-noun phrase, such as "bad cat", the former word ("bad") acts as an operator, i.e., *modifier*, to the latter word ("cat"), modifying its meaning. In (Baroni and Zamparelli, 2010; Baroni et al., 2014a), it was proposed that such modifications can be implemented via the use of functions that act as linear transformations in VSMs. Application of these functions is realized via matrix-by-vector multiplication as (Baroni et al., 2014a):

$$f(\alpha) =_{def} F \times a = b, \quad (5)$$

where F is the matrix-encoded function f, a is the vectorial representation of the argument α, and b is the compositional vector output. The F function is learnt according to examples of observed input and output (distributional) representations. The input is the representation of the head word, and the output is the representation of the phrase. Regression is employed for calculating the set of weights in the matrix that best approximate the observed vectors. For example, the function for the modifier "bad" is learnt by regressing over phrase examples and their head nouns, such as <*pet, bad pet*>, <*dog, bad dog*>, <*bird, bad bird*>. Using the trained set of weights and the vectorial representation of the head noun, e.g., "cat", the composite representation for the phrase "bad cat" is induced.

5.1 Fusion

The proposed network-based model, presented in Section 4, exploits the merging of word senses for computing activation areas for phrases. The model defined by (5) utilizes the transformational function of an operator for changing the meaning of a phrase. Both models (intuitively) seem to be aligned with the human process of phrase comprehension, however, there are cases that one of the models applies better than the other. Consider two example phrases, "football manager" and "successful engineer". The transformational model is expected to perform better for the latter phrase, while for the first phrase an intersection of word senses (i.e., a network-based model) seems to be more appropriate.

Based on the above considerations, we propose a fusion of the lexical function (*lf*), defined by (5), with the proposed network-based models. The fusion is aimed to model more accurately the semantic representations of complex structures. To do so, we measure the Mean Squared Error (MSE) when training the lexical function model, in order to quantify the transformative degree of the modifier under investigation. The transformative degree is used for deciding whether a network-based or a transformational model is more appropriate. Given two phrases, $i = (i_1\ i_2)$ and $j = (j_1\ j_2)$, the transformative degree $T(i, j)$ is defined as:

$$T(i, j) = \frac{1}{2}(MSE(i_1) + MSE(j_1)), \quad (6)$$

where $MSE(i_1)$ and $MSE(j_1)$ is the MSE that corresponds to modifiers i_1 and j_1, respectively. The proposed fusion metric, $\Phi^{lf}_{net}(i, j)$, used for estimating the similarity between the i and j phrases, is defined as:

$$\Phi^{lf}_{net}(i, j) = \lambda(i, j)\ S_N + (1 - \lambda(i, j))\ S_{LF}, \quad (7)$$

where S_N and S_{LF} are similarity scores computed by the network-based and lexical function models, respectively. λ is a function of i and j, computed using a sigmoid function as:

$$\lambda(i, j) = 0.5 / \left(1 + \mathrm{e}^{-T(i,j)}\right). \quad (8)$$

The sigmoid function is applied in order to smooth and normalize (within [0,1]) the values of $T(i, j)$.

Finally, in addition to the aforementioned fusion, we also implement a fusion combining the *lf* and the widely-used additive (*add*) (Mitchell and Lapata, 2008; Mitchell and Lapata, 2010) model. This fusion metric, Φ^{lf}_{add}, is defined similarly to (7).

6 Experiments and Evaluation

The procedure for creating the network and conducting the experiments is described in Section 6.1. In Section 6.2, we evaluate the proposed models and compare them with results from the literature.

6.1 Experimental Procedure

We defined our vocabulary (network nodes) by intersecting the English vocabulary found in the ASPELL[2] dictionary and the Wikipedia dump[3] to derive an English vocabulary of approximately 135K words. Using it, a corpus comprising of web-harvested document snippets was constructed by downloading 1000 snippets for each word in the vocabulary. Word-level similarities were computed among all vocabulary entries' pairs. To this end, the Normalized Google Distance (G) was utilized, proposed in (Vitanyi, 2005; Cilibrasi and Vitanyi, 2007) and motivated by Kolmogorov complexity. Let G be defined as

$$G(w_1, w_2) = \frac{\max\{A\} - \log|D|w_1, w_2|}{\log|D| - \min\{A\}}, \quad (9)$$

where w_1 and w_2 are two vocabulary words under investigation, $|D|$ is the total number of documents in the corpus, $|D|w_1, w_2|$ is the total number of documents containing both w_1 and w_2, and $A = \{\log|D|w_1|, \log|D|w_2|\}$. We used a variation of (9), proposed in (Gracia et al., 2006), referred to as "Google-based Semantic Relatedness" (G'). This variation defines a similarity measure, bounded within the $[0, 1]$ range and defined as

$$G'(w_1, w_2) = e^{-2G(w_1, w_2)}, \quad (10)$$

where $G(w_1, w_2)$ is computed according to (9). In this work, D denotes the sentence rather than the document, as the co-occurrence of words was defined at sentence-level. This metric was adopted based on its good performance in word-level semantic similarity tasks (Iosif and Potamianos, 2015).

Network-based model. We used sizes of $\theta = \{10, 25, 50, 100, 150, 500\}$ for the case of fixed-size neighborhoods, and $\theta = \{1, 5, ..., 40\}$ for the extended activation models described in Section 4.1. We used both the baseline and the extended activation layers for the M model, the latter being defined as M'. For M_k and P_k, we set $k = \{1, ..., 5\}$.

Transformational model. For the *lf* model described in (5), we computed co-occurence counts for bigrams occurring at least 50 times in the corpus. Positive Pointwise Mutual Information (PPMI) was applied to reweigh them. We used a) Singular Value Decomposition (SVD), and b) Non-Negative Matrix Factorization (NMF) (Lee and Seung, 2001) to reduce the dimensionality of the space down to a) 300, and b) 500 dimensions. To train *lf*, we selected corpus bigrams comprising of a *modifier* and a *noun*. We used a) Least Squares (LSR), and b) Ridge (RR) (Hastie et al., 2009) regression. The DIStributional SEmantics Composition Toolkit (DISSECT[4], (Dinu et al., 2013)) was used to implement *lf*, as well as the widely-used additive (*add*) and multiplicative (*mult*) models proposed in (Mitchell and Lapata, 2008; Mitchell and Lapata, 2010).

Fusion model. We combined the best performing model configurations on NNs (see Section 6.2) in order to implement the proposed fusion models.

6.2 Evaluation Results

For evaluation purposes, we used the widely-used Mitchell & Lapata (2010) datasets comprising of 108 noun-noun (NN), adjective-noun (AN), and verb-object (VO) phrase pairs, evaluated by human judgements and averaged per phrase pair. The models were evaluated using Spearman's correlation coefficient. Evaluation results are presented in Table 1. Due to space limitations, only the best performing network-based model configurations are reported here. Also, since the *mult* model performs poorly when the composed vectors contain negative values, as is the case with SVD, we only report results for the NMF variations for it. Finally, since training the *lf* model with RR had significantly superior performance over LSR in all configurations, we only report evaluations of the former.

The *lf* model, when using RR in combination with NMF, performs best (.76) for the case of NNs. Best performances for ANs and VOs are obtained by the *add* model (.63 and .59, respectively).

[2] http://www.aspell.net/

[3] As of the 4th quarter of 2012.

[4] http://clic.cimec.unitn.it/composes/toolkit/

Model	NN	AN	VO
add (NMF300)	**.67**	.61	.53
add (NMF500)	.66	**.63**	.56
add (SVD300)	.63	.59	**.59**
add (SVD500)	.66	**.63**	**.59**
mult (NMF300)	.59	.38	.36
mult (NMF500)	.59	.36	.42
lf (NMF300, RR)	**.76**	**.46**	**.35**
lf (NMF500, RR)	.67	.41	.28
lf (SVD300, RR)	.63	.35	.26
lf (SVD500, RR)	.56	.33	.23
M (Intersection)	.56	.46	.37
M' (Intersection)	.61	**.57**	**.47**
$M_{k=3}$ (Intersection)	**.64**	.51	.41
$P_{k=3}$ (Most-similar)	.63	.46	.23
H (Intersection)	.58	.39	.26
fusion Φ^{lf}_{net}	**.80**	.54	.35
fusion Φ^{lf}_{add}	.76	**.57**	**.44**

Table 1: Performance of models on NN, AN, and VO phrase pairs. Evaluations are reported using Spearman's correlation coefficient with human ratings.

Regarding network-based models, performance is improved when using the extended activation model over the baseline. This is confirmed by the absolute 5%, 11% and 10% increase for the case of NN, AN, and VO pairs, respectively, for the M metric. All the extended network-based models perform consistently better than the baseline of M, in the case of NNs, although their performance drops for the case of ANs and VOs. In the case of P_k, the scheme that constructs neighborhoods via the selection of the most similar neighbors performs better than the intersection- or the union-based scheme.

Φ^{lf}_{add} yields no relative improvements over the best performances of the separate models. Φ^{lf}_{net} provides an improvement for the case of NNs, reaching .80, which is also the best observed performance overall. However, Φ^{lf}_{net} does not improve performance in the case of ANs and VOs.

Performance improvements when using the extended activation layer for compositional structures is consistent with experimental observations from psycholinguistics (Osherson and Smith, 1981), and shows that the activation area for phrases might be adaptive to the degree of relatedness between words.

7 Discussion

The results displayed in Table 1 for the fusion models provide an indication of the different ways in which the operator changes the meaning of a phrase. In this section, we investigate the transformational properties of phrases as defined by their modifiers. By observing the properties of modifiers, we discuss whether their use in a phrase has mainly a *transformational* or a merely *compositional* effect, based on the goodness of fit of each model, estimated during model training.

7.1 The Transformative Effect of Modifiers

Early research on compositionality involved applying the word-level semantic similarity estimation techniques to phrases using context-based, bag-of-words models, i.e., defining the structures' meaning as a function of the words in their context. Though simple and cost-effective, the aforementioned techniques fail to detect the effect that a word has to its linguistic context and the semantic changes on its meaning, e.g., a "nice" table is still a table but a "fake" or "broken" table is not.

Depending on context, a modifier can affect the meaning of the encompassing phrase in different ways. For example, the modifier "normal" changes the meaning of "normal cat" much less than the modifier "dead" in "dead cat". Moreover, the modifier effect may vary for each syntactic category. For example, verbs can be transitive or intransitive, nouns can be abstract or concrete, and adjectives can be intensional or not (Boleda et al., 2013). Words that act as *functions* on their linguistic context have attracted much interest, and have recently been successfully handled by computational models.

7.2 Estimating the Transformative Degree

We categorise modifiers based on their regression performance, when training them for the *lf* model. Specifically, we acquire the MSE of their training as a measure for deciding the degree of their transformative effect on a given head noun. Taking the MSE is a sensible approach, since regression tries to derive a close approximation to observed vectorial representations of phrases and head nouns by means of transforming the head noun vector; high error in training indicates that the *lf* model is a poor match for this modifier. We trained the *lf* model using Ridge Regression and estimated the MSE for each modifier. In Table 2, we present example modifiers of low, neutral, and high transformative degree, as defined by their MSE score. We observe that highly-transformative modifiers have a more functional influence, when used in bigram structures. For example, in "efficient machine", "efficient" has a greater effect on the meaning of "efficient machine" rather than, e.g., "new" in "new machine". A "new machine" retains the same properties of a generic machine. However, an "efficient machine" should contain mechanisms that account for optimization of speed, cost, etc. Our observations suggest that modifiers affect the structure in which they occur in different ways. Some modifiers have a stronger effect on the meaning of the head noun, while others act merely as constituents of simple compositions. The proposed fusion of the transformational, *lf* model, with network-based or simple compositional models indicates that combining different models can yield improved performance when the transformative degree of modifiers is used as a fusion criterion.

Degree	Nouns	Adjectives	Verbs
Low	news	new	like
	service	great	buy
	business	black	help
	world	general	use
	state	good	provide
Neutral	company	various	face
	care	right	need
	community	better	cut
High	railway	old	encourage
	labour	rural	attend
	defence	elderly	remember
	personnel	efficient	satisfy
	committee	practical	suffer

Table 2: Examples of low, neutral, and high transformative modifiers.

8 Conclusions

We presented a network-based model that operates on neighborhoods of variable size to calculate similarity of compositional structures. We investigated various methods for composing neighborhoods of adjacent words and presented three metrics, motivated by psycholinguistics and metric space algebra, for estimating similarity between activation areas. Employing variable size activation improves semantic similarity performance, revealing a different activational behavior among bigrams. We also presented a fusion of the proposed models with the lexical function model based on the transformative degree of modifiers, achieving an improvement of performance for noun-noun compositions, reaching state-of-the-art performance of 80% Spearman correlation with human judgements. We further investigated the transformative degree of modifiers, and elaborated on their role as mostly *compositional* or *transformational*.

In future work, we will further investigate the role of modifiers and their application in the proposed activation composition approaches, while also explore the criteria for deriving activations and deciding on fusion strategies. We also plan to apply network-based models on longer semantic structures.

Acknowledgments

This work has been partially funded by the SpeDial project supported by the EU FP7 with grant number 611396, and the BabyAffect project supported by the Greek General Secretariat for Research and Technology (GSRT) with grant number 3610.

References

Eneko Agirre, Daniel Cer, Mona Diab, and Aitor Gonzalez-Agirre. 2012. Semeval-2012 task 6: A pilot on semantic textual similarity. In *Proceedings of the 6th International Workshop on Semantic Evaluation (SemEval 2012), in conjuction with the First Joint Conference on Lexical and Computational Semantic (*SEM 2012)*, pages 385–393.

Eneko Agirre, Daniel Cer, Mona Diab, Aitor Gonzalez-Agirre, and Weiwei Guo. 2013. Sem 2013 shared task: Semantic textual similarity, including a pilot on typed-similarity. In *In* SEM 2013: The Second Joint Conference on Lexical and Computational Semantics. Association for Computational Linguistics.*

Ion Androutsopoulos and Prodromos Malakasiotis. 2010. A survey of paraphrasing and textual entailment methods. *Journal of Artificial Intelligence Research*, 38:135–187.

Marco Baroni and Alessandro Lenci. 2010. Distributional memory: A general framework for corpus-based semantics. *Computational Linguistics*, 36(4):673–721.

Marco Baroni and Roberto Zamparelli. 2010. Nouns are vectors, adjectives are matrices: Representing adjective-noun constructions in semantic space. In *Proceedings of EMNLP 2010*, pages 1183–1193.

Marco Baroni, Raffaela Bernardi, and Roberto Zamparelli. 2014a. Frege in space: A program of compositional distributional semantics. *Linguistic Issues in Language Technology (LiLT)*, 9.

Marco Baroni, Georgiana Dinu, and Germán Kruszewski. 2014b. Dont count, predict! A systematic comparison of context-counting vs. context-predicting semantic vectors. In *Proceedings of the 52nd Annual Meeting of the Association for Computational Linguistics*, volume 1, pages 238–247.

Yoshua Bengio, Réjean Ducharme, and Pascal Vincent. 2003. A neural probabilistic language model. *Journal of Machine Learning Research*, 3:1137–1155.

Gemma Boleda, Marco Baroni, Nghia T. Pham, and Louise McNally. 2013. Intensionality was only alleged: On adjective-noun composition in distributional semantics. In *Proceedings of IWCS 2013*, pages 35–46.

Rudi L. Cilibrasi and Paul MB Vitanyi. 2007. The Google similarity distance. *IEEE Transactions on Knowledge and Data Engineering*, 19(3):370–383.

Georgiana Dinu, Nghia The Pham, and Marco Baroni. 2013. DISSECT-DIStributional SEmantics Composition Toolkit. In *Proceedings of the 51st Annual Meeting of ACL: System Demonstrations*, pages 31–36.

Jorge Gracia, Raquel Trillo, Mauricio Espinoza, and Eduardo Mena. 2006. Querying the web: A multiontology disambiguation method. In *Proceedings of the 6th International Conference on Web Engineering (ICWE 2006)*, pages 241–248.

Gregory Grefenstette. 1994. *Explorations in Automatic Thesaurus Discovery*. Kluwer Academic Publishers.

Zellig Harris. 1954. Distributional structure. *Word*, 10(23):146–162.

Trevor Hastie, Robert Tibshirani, and Jerome Friedman. 2009. *The Elements of Statistical Learning*, volume 2. Springer.

Wen-Liang Hung and Miin-Shen Yang. 2004. Similarity measures of intuitionistic fuzzy sets based on hausdorff distance. *Pattern Recognition Letters*, 25(14):1603–1611.

Elias Iosif and Alexandros Potamianos. 2015. Similarity computation using semantic networks created from web-harvested data. *Natural Language Engineering*, 21(01):49–79.

Elias Iosif. 2013. *Network-based Distributional Semantic Models*. Ph.D. thesis, Technical University of Crete, Chania, Greece.

Daniel D. Lee and Sebastian H. Seung. 2001. Algorithms for non-negative matrix factorization. In *Advances in Neural Information Processing Systems*, pages 556–562.

Nikolaos Malandrakis, Alexandros Potamianos, Elias Iosif, and Shrikanth Narayanan. 2013. Distributional semantic models for affective text analysis. *IEEE Transactions on Audio, Speech, and Language Processing*, 21(11):2379–2392.

T. P. McNamara. 2005. *Semantic Priming: Perspectives from Memory and Word Recognition*. Psychology Press.

Tomas Mikolov, Kai Chen, Greg Corrado, and Jeffrey Dean. 2013. Efficient estimation of word representations in vector space. *ICLR Workshop*.

Jeff Mitchell and Mirella Lapata. 2008. Vector-based models of semantic composition. In *Proceedings of ACL*, pages 236–244.

Jeff Mitchell and Mirella Lapata. 2010. Composition in distributional models of semantics. *Cognitive science*, 34(8):1388–1429.

Daniel N. Osherson and Edward E. Smith. 1981. On the adequacy of prototype theory as a theory of concepts. *Cognition*, 9(1):35–58.

Francis J. Pelletier. 1994. The principle of semantic compositionality. *Topoi*, 13(1):11–24.

Tamara Polajnar, Laura Rimell, and Stephen Clark. 2014. Evaluation of simple distributional compositional operations on longer texts. In *9th Language Resources and Evaluation Conference (LREC 2014)*.

Richard Socher, Brody Huval, Christopher D. Manning, and Andrew Y. Ng. 2012. Semantic compositionality through recursive matrix-vector spaces. In *Proceedings of EMNLP-CoNLL*, pages 1201–1211.

Peter D. Turney and Patrick Pantel. 2010. From frequency to meaning: Vector space models of semantics. *Journal of Artificial Intelligence Research*, 37(1):141–188.

Peter D. Turney. 2012. Domain and function: A dual-space model of semantic relations and compositions. *Journal of Artificial Intelligence Research*, 44:533–585.

Paul Vitanyi. 2005. Universal similarity. In *Proceedings of Information Theory Workshop on Coding and Complexity*, pages 238–243.

Verb polysemy and frequency effects in thematic fit modeling

Clayton Greenberg, Vera Demberg, and Asad Sayeed
Computational Linguistics and Phonetics / M[2]CI Cluster of Excellence
Saarland University
66123 Saarbrücken, Germany
{claytong,vera,asayeed}@coli.uni-saarland.de

Abstract

While several data sets for evaluating thematic fit of verb-role-filler triples exist, they do not control for verb polysemy. Thus, it is unclear how verb polysemy affects human ratings of thematic fit and how best to model that. We present a new dataset of human ratings on high vs. low-polysemy verbs matched for verb frequency, together with high vs. low-frequency and well-fitting vs. poorly-fitting patient role-fillers. Our analyses show that low-polysemy verbs produce stronger thematic fit judgements than verbs with higher polysemy. Role-filler frequency, on the other hand, had little effect on ratings. We show that these results can best be modeled in a vector space using a clustering technique to create multiple prototype vectors representing different "senses" of the verb.

1 Introduction

Being able to accurately estimate thematic fit (e.g., is *cake* a good patient of *cut*?) can be useful both for a wide range of NLP applications and for cognitive models of human language processing difficulty, as human processing difficulty is highly sensitive to semantic plausibilities (Ehrlich and Rayner, 1981).

Previous studies obtained quantitative thematic fit data by asking human participants to rate how common, plausible, typical, or appropriate some test role-fillers are for given verbs on a scale from 1 (least plausible) to 7 (most plausible) (McRae et al., 1998; Binder et al., 2001; Padó, 2007; Padó et al., 2009; Vandekerckhove et al., 2009). For example, as part of the McRae et al. (1998) dataset, the thematic fit of the noun "principal" as the patient of the verb "dismiss" is 2.0 out of 7.0. As an agent, its rating is 6.3. The McRae et al. (1998) dataset has a total of 720 verb-noun pairs (146 different verbs) with typicality ratings. The Padó (2007) dataset includes 18 verbs as well as up to twelve nominal arguments, totalling 207 verb-noun pairs. The verbs and nouns were chosen based on their frequent occurrence in the Penn Treebank and FrameNet.

While these datasets are very useful, e.g. for evaluating automatic systems for estimating thematic fit via correlations with these human judgements, they do not systematically vary polysemy of verbs or frequency of role-fillers. Further, it is unclear what effect polysemy and frequency have on thematic fit judgements. We thus ask: (1) are thematically well-fitting role-fillers for more polysemous verbs (e.g., "execute killer" or "execute will") judged to be equally well-fitting as thematically well-fitting role-fillers for less polysemous verbs ("jail criminal")? (2) Is a prototypical role-filler of a polysemous verb's less-frequent sense judged to be equally well-fitting as a prototypical role-filler of the verb's more frequent sense? (3) Finally, will a well-fitting but less frequent role-filler obtain the same rating as a more frequent but similarly-fitting role-filler?

The answers to these questions have implications for modeling thematic fit. An increasingly common method for determining the fit between a verb and its argument involves calculating typical role-fillers of that verb, calculating a centroid (or average) over the most typical role-fillers in a vector space model, and then calculating the similarity between the centroid

Proceedings of CMCL 2015, pages 48–57,
Denver, Colorado, June 4, 2015.

and the proposed role-filler via a similarity measure. Arguments that have high similarities with the prototypical centroid vector representing most common role-fillers for a given verb-role combination are then asserted to have good thematic fit (Baroni and Lenci, 2010; Erk, 2012).

This conceptualization, however, assumes that there is a single type of most typical filler for a role and that all good fillers will be distributionally similar. This assumption leads to problems when this process is to be applied to ambiguous verbs; when a verb has many different senses, there can exist typical role-fillers for each sense which are all highly suitable role-fillers for the given role but are distributionally very different from one another. This means that the calculated prototypical role-filler will be a mixture of the arguments that are typical role-fillers for the main senses of the verb.

Greenberg et al. (2015) addressed this problem by clustering the most common role-fillers in order to represent the prototypes of each of the verb senses. They found that better correlations with human judgements on the Padó (2007) and McRae et al. (1998) datasets are achieved when calculating the maximal cosine similarity for a candidate role-filler with respect to the prototypical role-fillers of each word sense.

Thus, their model represents the similarity to the most similar prototype role-filler, which means that a good role-filler of an infrequent verb sense could get the same level of ratings as a good role-filler of a frequent verb sense. There exists, however, currently no data to assess whether this is desirable behavior, or whether we, in fact, need a model that calculates similarity to prototypical role-fillers *and* takes into account verb sense frequencies.

2 Thematic fit modeling

Quantifications of thematic fit are a ternary relation between a verb, a semantic role, and a role-filler. For example, given human judges, we would expect *cake* to be a highly-rated patient-filler of *cut*, but we would expect *cake* to be a poorly-rated agent-filler of *cut*. There have been multiple attempts to model thematic fit judgements. The goal is generally to estimate a probability for a thematic role-filler given a verb and a role. However, due to data sparseness, it is not possible to estimate this probability directly. Existing approaches estimate a candidate noun's thematic fit via its similarity to typical role-fillers that have been observed. Similarity between the candidate noun and prototypical fillers is thereby assessed via WordNet classes (e.g., Resnik, 1996; Padó et al., 2009), or by cosine similarities in a vector space model (e.g., Baroni and Lenci, 2010; Erk, 2012). However, vector space methods achieve better coverage than WordNet class methods (Erk et al., 2010).

In vector-space modeling approaches like the one used in this paper, the calculation of a thematic fit for a verb-role-noun triple proceeds though the identification of a prototype vector of a verb's role-fillers. The prototype vector is constructed from the representations of words that are previously known to be typical role-fillers for that verb. For example, we might identify typical patient-fillers of *cut* to be *meat*, *budget*, *paper*, and so on. A geometric measure such as cosine similarity is used to compare the vector for the candidate role-filler with the prototype vector.

2.1 Distributional memory vector space models

The models evaluated in this paper (TypeDM, SDDM, and SDDMX) are based on the distributional memory (DM) framework originally promulgated by Baroni and Lenci (2010). DM is a generalized, broad-coverage, unsupervised model for representing linguistic relationships in a very high-dimensional vector space. A DM is an order 3 tensor, two of whose axes are words and one of whose axes is a syntactic or semantic link between words. In other words, a cell of a DM represents a tuple $< w_1, \text{link}, w_2 >$, and the value contained in that cell is an adjusted frequency count—here, local mutual information (LMI; $O_{FRV} \log \frac{O_{FRV}}{E_{FRV}}$, where O and E are the observed and expected frequencies of filler F, role R, and verb V appearing together). Using a structured vector space model is crucial for modeling thematic fit (as we need to distinguish between explicit roles, e.g. typical agents vs. patients of a verb).

The **TypeDM** model[1] (Baroni and Lenci, 2010) is constructed from the ukWaC, BNC, and WaCkype-

[1]Available at `http://clic.cimec.unitn.it/dm/`.

dia corpora. In TypeDM, the links represent both connections between words in the corpora found via the dependency parser MaltParser (Nivre et al., 2007) and further semantic dependencies derived from these connections via hand-crafted rules.

An alternative way of constructing DMs was proposed by Sayeed and Demberg (2014), where links between words are derived directly from SENNA, a neural network-based semantic role labeller (Collobert and Weston, 2007; Collobert et al., 2011). This DM is called SENNA-DepDM, or **SDDM** for short in this paper. Unlike TypeDM, the links in this tensor are not processed by hand-crafted rules.

SDDMX[2] is a version of SDDM with one expansion: it includes additional links between role-fillers that are found to be related via a verb. Both SDDM and SDDMX are trained on ukWaC and the BNC.

Greenberg et al. (2015) tested TypeDM, SDDM, and SDDMX on multiple datasets of human judgements for agent, patient, location, and instrument roles. They used multiple models and datasets because robustness of trends across these different configurations lends support to their generality. They found that the methods tested had comparable performance across the three models, with TypeDM outperforming considerably on the McRae et al. (1998) agent/patient dataset and SDDMX likewise on locations. We included TypeDM, SDDM, and SDDMX in our experimental evaluation on the new dataset to allow similar cross-model analysis.

2.2 Modeling verb senses

While prior vector space models for thematic fit have ignored verb polysemy, Greenberg et al. (2015) recently proposed to partition the "typical" role-fillers of a verb like "observe" such that each partition reflects typical role-fillers of separate senses of the verb.

In that work, they compared the traditional method of representing a prototypical role-filler by calculating a single $Centroid$ from a verb's 20 highest-LMI role-fillers with three other thematic fit estimation methods: $OneBest$, in which the cosine is taken separately with all of the 20 highest-LMI fillers and the best cosine is reported; $2Clusters$, in which the 20 fillers are partitioned into two clusters and the best fit is taken from the corresponding prototypes; and $kClusters$, in which the 20 fillers are dynamically partitioned into three or more clusters using NLTK's (Bird et al., 2009) group-average agglomerative clustering package and using the Variance Ratio Criterion (Caliński and Harabasz, 1974) as a stopping criterion for partitioning. They concluded that variable clustering ($kClusters$) provides gains in thematic fit modeling over the other methods, suggesting a need to take into account verb polysemy with respect to thematic roles in order to model human judgements more accurately. Also, since their clustering methods helped patients much more than agents, they successfully reproduced the previously known notion that patients are more specific to individual senses of a verb than agents.

3 Methods and stimuli

In this work, we describe a novel dataset of thematic fit judgements that systematically varies verb polysemy and role-filler frequency. Then, we evaluate the automatic thematic fit estimation methods from Greenberg et al. (2015) on this dataset. If verb polysemy and filler frequency can be shown to affect human thematic fit judgements, these results would suggest certain desirable traits for automatic systems and provide evidence for or against the claims made by Greenberg et al. (2015). In addition to whether the factors of polysemy and frequency are associated with shifts in the rating scale, we also would like to know how these shifts change at both scale extrema, whether good role-fillers of different verb senses receive relatively equal ratings, and how an automatic thematic fit estimation system with prototype clustering handles different types of verbs with respect to these manipulations.

We begin with the necessary evil of operationalizing polysemy. It is probably impossible to prove without a doubt that a certain verb has only one meaning, usage, etc. However, a binary classification between less polysemous and more polysemous verbs is certainly attainable, even if the boundary is not beyond reproach. For our purposes, we will define a verb as MONOSEMOUS if its lemma is a member of only one SynSet in WordNet (Fellbaum, 1998). Hence, a verb is POLYSEMOUS if its lemma

[2]SDDM, SDDMX, and this paper's dataset are available at http://rollen.mmci.uni-saarland.de/.

is a member of more than one SynSet in WordNet. A possible confound when manipulating polysemy is verb frequency, as higher frequency words in general tend to be more polysemous. We control for verb frequency by selecting POLYSEMOUS verbs to match the frequency of the MONOSEMOUS verbs in our dataset as much as possible. Furthermore, we systematically vary the frequency of the role-fillers, i.e., selecting a high and low frequency noun in each condition.

3.1 Task format and template

Since Greenberg et al. (2015) were able to confirm that patients are more specific to individual senses of a verb than agents, we decided to focus on patient role-fillers in our new dataset, thus emphasizing the effects of polysemy. For patient-fillers, both McRae et al. (1998) and Padó (2007) used questions of the form *"How common is it for a NOUN to be VERB-ed?"* to elicit judgements for their datasets. But consider the example: *"How common is it for croquet to be played?"* Since croquet is not a very common game, we would expect the rating in response to this question to be relatively low. But, intuitively, *croquet* is an excellent patient-filler for *play*. So, instead, we decided to ask participants to rate how much they agree with statements of the form *"A NOUN is something that is VERB-ed"* (template for non-human patient-fillers) and *"A NOUN is someone who is VERB-ed"* (template for human patient-fillers) on a Likert scale from 1 (never) to 7 (always). We chose this construction as our template because it does not use any technical terms and avoids conflating absolute frequency of the verb with conditional probability of the patient-filler, e.g. croquet is always something that is played, so it should receive a high rating.

3.2 Selection of experimental items

Given that MONOSEMOUS verbs are far less plentiful than POLYSEMOUS ones, we first selected the MONOSEMOUS verbs. To start, we filtered the 500,000 most frequent tokens in COCA (Davies, 2008) for parts of speech starting with `v` (verbs sorted by descending frequency). Then, using the WordNet lemmatizer as part of NLTK (Bird et al., 2009), we lemmatized the verbs, combined the duplicate entries that arose from multiple inflected forms, and then filtered out all lemmata that were part of multiple SynSets. The top 48 most frequent MONOSEMOUS verbs that were acceptable in our template constructions were compiled into a list. These vary in frequency from "thank" (82987 occurrences) down to "sample" (1275 occurrences).

Then, by querying COCA with the trigram *VERB* `[at*] [nn*]`, we obtained a list of excerpts from the corpus in which the verb was followed by a determiner (article) and then a noun. This targeted patient-fillers, since in English, they usually appear right after the verb. Therefore, the results of this query formed a list of candidate patient-fillers sorted by cooccurrence frequency. One particularly well-fitting patient-filler was selected from this list, giving priority to the higher (more frequent) entries. After this, using Roget's 21st Century Thesaurus accessed through `http://www.thesaurus.com`, we selected a very similar but less frequent version of the patient-filler. The relevant unigram patient-filler frequencies were obtained by querying a version of the 500,000 most frequent tokens in COCA that was filtered for only nouns and lemmatized using the WordNet lemmatizer as part of NLTK. The median ratio of the high frequency patient-fillers to their low frequency counterparts was 9.912.

Once the MONOSEMOUS verbs were finalized, we compiled the POLYSEMOUS verbs. First, we generated the same list from which the MONOSEMOUS verbs were selected, except that instead of filtering out lemmata that were part of more than one SynSet, we filtered out lemmata that were part of fewer than three SynSets. While this is stronger than our initial definition of POLYSEMOUS, we wanted to make sure that polysemy is effectively manipulated. Then, beginning at the frequency of each MONOSEMOUS verb, we looked for a verb as close in frequency as possible to that MONOSEMOUS verb that had at least two significantly contrasting, transitive senses according to experimenter intuition, confirmed by corresponding SynSets in WordNet, giving priority to verbs that were members of many SynSets. The median number of WordNet SynSets belonging to each of these 48 POLYSEMOUS verbs was 7. The frequencies of the POLYSEMOUS verbs varied from "started" (80898 occurrences) down to "scratched" (1465 occurrences).

The same format trigram COCA queries aided this POLYSEMOUS verb selection process as well as the selection of a high frequency good patient-filler for each of two senses. Priority was still given to those nouns with greatest cooccurrence with the verb, but the two-sense requirement made this more difficult. Low frequency versions of these good patient-fillers were analogously selected using the thesaurus. The more frequent of the two experimental senses of these POLYSEMOUS verbs, according to SynSet ordering in WordNet, was labelled as `Sense1` and the less frequent was labelled `Sense2`. The median ratio of the high frequency patient-fillers to their low frequency counterparts was 7.335 for `Sense1` and 10.288 for `Sense2`.

To investigate multiplicative as well as additive adjustments to the thematic fit rating scale, we needed to determine bad patient-fillers explicitly. For this we randomly shuffled the good role-fillers for the MONOSEMOUS verbs and paired them with each MONOSEMOUS verb again. If the thematic fit of a randomly assigned pair of bad patient-fillers was too good, possibly because the verb had coincidently been paired with its good patient-fillers again, a swap was made. To ensure that polysemy and other idiosyncrasies of the selected patient-fillers for MONOSEMOUS verbs were controlled, we used a random ordering of the patient-fillers for the MONOSEMOUS verbs also as the bad patient-fillers for the POLYSEMOUS verbs. Once again, swaps were made if the thematic fit of a randomly assigned pair of bad patient-fillers was too good. Note that another way to obtain bad role-fillers would have been to invert the animacy and/or concreteness of the good role-fillers. However, since this study is concerned with scalar thematic fit judgements as opposed to hard classifications, we thought that the variation in thematic fit arising from randomly selecting bad fillers would be more appropriate.

To summarize the experimental items, this dataset has 48 MONOSEMOUS verbs each with frequency-contrasting pairs of good and bad patient-fillers. Also it has 48 POLYSEMOUS verbs each with frequency-contrasting pairs of good patient-fillers for `Sense1`, good patient-fillers for `Sense2`, and bad patient-fillers. In Table 1, we show the selected patient-fillers for the POLYSEMOUS verb *whip* and the MONOSEMOUS verb *punish*.

Filler type	**Frequency**	*whip*	*punish*
`Sense1`	high	horse	criminal
	low	stallion	outlaw
`Sense2`	high	cream	-
	low	frosting	-
`Bad`	high	party	baby
	low	gathering	fetus

Table 1: Example items from our thematic fit dataset.

3.3 Fillers

In order to evaluate consistency with the *"How common is it..."* format and also to identify excessively divergent responses, we adapted 240 (patient-filler, verb) pairs from McRae et al. (1998) as a counterpart to our novel experimental items. To select these pairs, we excluded all verbs that appeared as experimental items, scored each remaining pair using the sum of the COCA unigram frequencies of the verb and patient-filler, and selected the 240 highest scoring pairs. Note that because of this procedure, the verbs that were selected as fillers did not necessarily appear with all of their role-fillers from the McRae et al. (1998) dataset.

3.4 Experimental setup

In order to prepare the 480 total (patient-filler, verb) pairs for inclusion in a human experiment, we rewrote each verb by hand in its past participle form and each patient-filler by hand in its singular form with an appropriate (possibly null) determiner. Also, each patient-filler was hand tagged with a `+human` or `-human` feature. That way, each (patient-filler, verb) pair could be felicitously entered into the non-human-filler template or the human-filler template.

We obtained participants for this study using Amazon Mechanical Turk. For a survey consisting of six POLYSEMOUS items, four MONOSEMOUS items, and five filler items, counterbalanced for condition and question order, a worker was paid \$0.15. Workers were restricted such that they were not allowed to rate a verb in more than one condition. So, each worker could complete a maximum of eight surveys. A total of 159 workers participated, and each sentence was rated by 10 different workers.

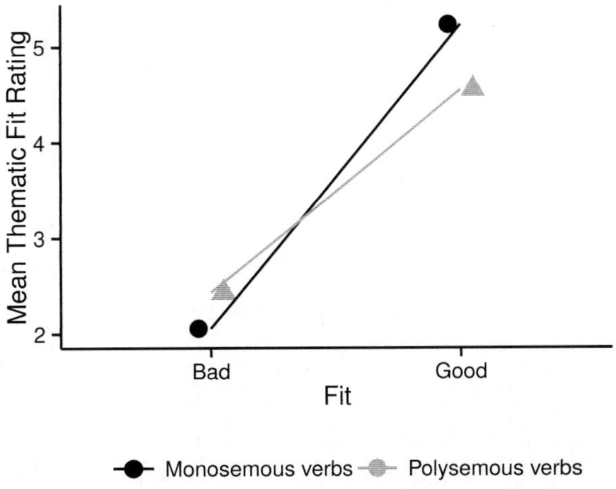

Figure 1: Interaction between Fit and $Polysemy$.

4 Results

The Spearman's ρ correlation between the human judgements we obtained on our filler items and the human judgements obtained by McRae et al. (1998) is 0.753.

Our highest level experimental analysis was a factorial ANOVA with "hc3" correction as suggested by Long and Ervin (2000), which had three, between participant, binary factors: $Polysemy$, experimenter judgement (Fit), and *Frequency* (binned). This analysis provided two important results. First, it empirically confirmed the choices of our experimental patient-fillers, which were designed to fit either very well or poorly. This effect of Fit was significant and very large: $F(1, 4668) = 3029.692$, $p < 2 \times 10^{-16}$, $\eta_p^2 = 0.394$.

Second, there was a significant $Polysemy * Fit$ interaction, summarized visually in Figure 1, $F(1, 4668) = 125.729$, $p < 2 \times 10^{-16}$, $\eta_p^2 = 0.026$. Namely, for POLYSEMOUS verbs, bad patient-fillers were not as bad (POLYSEMOUS: $M = 2.43$, $SD = 1.56$ versus MONOSEMOUS: $M = 2.06$, $SD = 1.38$) and good patient-fillers were not as good (POLYSEMOUS: $M = 4.55$, $SD = 1.65$ versus MONOSEMOUS: $M = 5.23$, $SD = 1.44$). We used two-tailed Welch t-tests on both bad patient-fillers, $t(1813.212) = 5.4756$, $p = 4.968 \times 10^{-8}$, Cohen's $d = 0.173$, and good patient-fillers, $t(2139.706) = 11.3243$, $p < 2.2 \times 10^{-16}$, Cohen's $d = 0.272$, to confirm that these differences were significant. Finally, we found significant, but very small, main effects of $Polysemy$, $F(1, 4668) = 16.175$, $p = 5.87 \times 10^{-5}$, $\eta_p^2 = 0.003$, and also $Frequency$, $F(1, 4668) = 11.184$, $p = 0.000832$, $\eta_p^2 = 0.002$ on how people generally rated thematic fit.

Then, we ran four follow-up 2×2 factorial ANOVAs with "hc3" correction, each holding a $Polysemy$ or Fit condition constant. First, for good patient-fillers, both $Polysemy$, $F(1, 2830) = 117.761$, $p < 2 \times 10^{-16}$, $\eta_p^2 = 0.040$, and $Frequency$, $F(1, 2830) = 8.670$, $p = 0.00326$, $\eta_p^2 = 0.003$ were significant. Second, for bad patient-fillers, $Polysemy$ was significant, $F(1, 1838) = 29.997$, $p = 4.92 \times 10^{-8}$, $\eta_p^2 = 0.016$, but *Frequency* was not, $F(1, 1838) = 2.524$, $p = 0.112$, $\eta_p^2 = 0.001$. That *Frequency* has a significant effect on good role-fillers but not on bad ones makes intuitive sense. After all, a less frequent version of a poorly-fitting role-filler should fit poorly to approximately the same degree.

Third, for POLYSEMOUS verbs, Fit was significant, $F(1, 2803) = 1054.885$, $p < 2 \times 10^{-16}$, $\eta_p^2 = 0.273$, but *Frequency* was not, $F(1, 2803) = 2.866$, $p = 0.0906$, $\eta_p^2 = 0.001$. Fourth, for MONOSEMOUS verbs, both Fit, $F(1, 1865) = 2373.263$, $p < 2 \times 10^{-16}$, $\eta_p^2 = 0.560$, and $Frequency$, $F(1, 1865) = 11.105$, $p = 0.000878$, $\eta_p^2 = 0.006$, were significant. That *Frequency* has a significant effect on MONOSEMOUS verbs but not on POLYSEMOUS ones appears to be indicative of a characteristic of low polysemy. These verbs produce such a strong expectation for certain role-fillers that even role-fillers that are semantically very similar but less frequent are deemed worse-fitting. POLYSEMOUS verbs, on the other hand, are more flexible than MONOSEMOUS verbs for fitting with less frequent role-fillers.

While verb frequency was very closely controlled in our stimuli via experimental design, we also ran a linear mixed effects model with thematic fit as a response variable and POLYSEMY*FIT+LOGVERBFREQ+FREQUENCY as predictors (with random intercepts under participant and item, as well as random slopes for POLYSEMY and FIT under both participants and items). The linear mixed effects model confirmed all results from the factorial ANOVAs, and furthermore

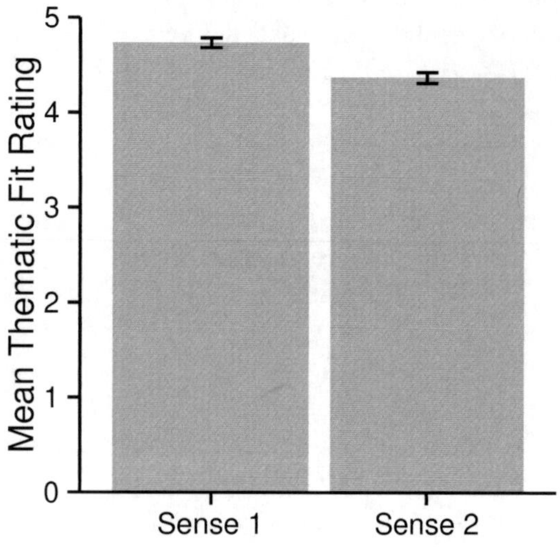

Figure 2: More frequent vs. less frequent senses of POLYSEMOUS verbs.

showed that our matching of verb frequencies in the experimental design was effective: LOGVERBFREQ did not explain away the effects of verb polysemy.

Next, we compared good patient-fillers for the two predetermined senses for the POLYSEMOUS verbs. A Factorial ANOVA with "hc3" correction and with *Sense* and *Frequency* as between participant factors indicated that there was a significant main effect of *Sense*, $F(1, 1881) = 23.076$, $p = 1.68 \times 10^{-6}$, $\eta_p^2 = 0.012$. Neither *Frequency*, $F(1, 1881) = 3.024$, $p = 0.0822$, $\eta_p^2 = 0.002$, nor the $Sense * Frequency$ interaction, $F(1, 1881) = 1.386$, $p = 0.2392$, $\eta_p^2 = 0.001$ was significant. A two-tailed Welch t-test confirmed that good patient-fillers for the more frequent sense of these POLYSEMOUS verbs were rated significantly higher ($M = 4.73$, $SD = 1.58$) than good patient-fillers for the less frequent sense ($M = 4.37$, $SD = 1.70$), $t(1868.449) = 4.7985$, $p = 1.725 \times 10^{-6}$, Cohen's $d = 0.254$, as shown in Figure 2. Therefore, while the unigram frequencies of the patient-fillers do not have an impact when comparing senses of the same verb, the frequencies of the senses themselves do have an effect.

Finally, in Table 2, we give the results of running the four automatic thematic fit scoring methods from Greenberg et al. (2015) on SDDM, SDDMX, and TypeDM and calculating the correlation with the human judgements we obtained on the experimental (role-filler, verb) pairs. For the *kClusters* method, 10 was set as the maximum number of clusters. In Table 3 we break down the TypeDM correlations by verb type. Note that the ALL column in Table 3 includes the filler items, but Table 2 does not.

	SDDM	SDDMX	TypeDM
Centroid	0.406	0.448	0.528
2Clusters	0.448	0.476	0.539
OneBest	0.509	0.531	0.544
kClusters	0.520	0.535	0.548

Table 2: Spearman's ρ values for correlation with MTurk judgements on experimental items.

	POLY.	MONO.	FILLERS	ALL
Centroid	0.405	0.655	0.313	0.464
2Clusters	0.442	0.642	0.311	0.474
OneBest	0.447	0.641	0.223	0.452
kClusters	0.432	0.669	0.304	0.479

Table 3: Spearman's ρ values for TypeDM correlation with MTurk judgements by verb type.

5 Discussion

The reasonably high correlation between our human judgements and those from McRae et al. (1998) is encouraging and provides a possible upper-bound on computational models of thematic fit as well as a human annotator agreement score for our study.

Since the *Fit* factor was experimentally designed to have an effect on ratings, it is unsurprising that there was an effect. But it is surprising that the *Polysemy* and *Frequency* effect sizes are much smaller than those of *Fit* and the interaction. This suggests that humans do not have such a varying process for assessing thematic fit for POLYSEMOUS versus MONOSEMOUS verbs. Therefore, these judgements further motivate clustering as part of an automatic thematic fit scoring system because clustering minimizes the effects of highly contrastive senses.

Overall, the interaction between *Polysemy* and *Fit* showed that in the case of POLYSEMOUS verbs, it is harder to achieve extremely low or high thematic fit. Only one sense needs to be relevant for a role-filler to achieve a somewhat high score, but the inability to fit well with all senses may block a good role-filler from achieving the highest possible score.

For the comparison of the two experimental senses for the POLYSEMOUS verbs, it is important to note a terminological subtlety. Our *Frequency* factor, which was found not to have a significant effect, is based on the *unigram* frequency of the role-filler, while the *Sense* factor, which was found to have a significant effect, is based on the relative frequency of that sense, which could be estimated using the (skip) *bigram* frequency of the verb with the role-filler. Since these bigram frequencies affect thematic fit ratings, automatic thematic fit estimation systems that analyze the frequency distribution of senses are likely to perform better than those that do not.

Table 2 reproduces the trends in correlations observed in Greenberg et al. (2015) on our new dataset. Again, we see that the trends occur on each of the DM models, which shows their generality. But, by breaking down the dataset by verb type, we can see a clearer picture of the strengths and weakness of the different scoring methods. For instance, the *OneBest* method achieves the best performance on POLYSEMOUS verbs, but worsens performance on MONOSEMOUS verbs. We can attribute this difference to a trade-off between negative impacts of polysemy and noise. Namely, for MONOSEMOUS verbs, the negative impact of noise is greater than the negative impact of polysemy, and vice versa for POLYSEMOUS verbs. Clustering, however, achieves the greatest correlation with human judgements on mixed polysemy datasets presumably by avoiding the greater negative effect for each verb.

As an example, consider the MONOSEMOUS verb *obey*. *kClusters* put the patient-fillers of *obey* into nine clusters: [[*injunction*], [*will*], [*wish*], [*limit*], [*equation*], [*master*], [*law, rule, commandment, principle, regulation, teaching, convention*], [*voice, word*], [*order, command, instruction, call, summons*]]. Due to a large number of singleton clusters, each cluster is quite pure. Hence, the noise has been neutralized. Similar role-fillers are still smoothed together, but no strongly dissimilar ones are averaged.

In contrast, *kClusters* put the patient-fillers for the POLYSEMOUS verb *observe* into six clusters: [[*day*], [*silence*], [*difference, change*], [*object, star, bird*], [*effect, phenomenon, pattern, behaviour, practice, behavior, reaction, movement, trend*], [*rule, custom, law, condition*]]. Now, there are only two singleton clusters, and the largest cluster is quite noisy. Each of the clusters except the largest happens to correspond uniquely to a WordNet SynSet, so the polysemy has been addressed, but not the noise. However, polysemy was more important than noise for this verb. We also note that the number of clusters, usually between six and nine, is not particularly informative about polysemy and has much more to do with noise in the set.

Finally, to explain the sharp discrepancy in performance between fillers and experimental items, recall that our main experiment had three independent variables: *Polysemy*, *Frequency*, and *Fit*. Both levels of *Polysemy* enjoyed the same positive effect when moving from the *Centroid* to *kClusters*. *Frequency* had a very small effect. This just leaves *Fit*. For each of our experimental verbs, we ensured that there was a pair of good role-fillers and a pair of bad role-fillers. The McRae et al. (1998) dataset did not ensure that there was a mix of good and bad role-fillers for each verb. Additionally, our filler item selection procedure did not always include every available role-filler for a given verb. If the selected role-fillers are either all good or all bad, these points "vote", during the Spearman's ρ calculation, to minimize all distinctions (good and bad) that the model makes. The more of these verbs we have, the flatter our model becomes and the less we will be able to see. But, none of our experimental items had this problem.

6 Conclusions and Future Work

We developed a new substantial dataset of thematic fit judgements: 720 verb-noun pairs, each judged by 10 Amazon Mechanical Turk workers. Our dataset contains 48 MONOSEMOUS and 48 POLYSEMOUS verbs, matched for frequency. For each of the POLYSEMOUS verbs, it has a total of six patient-fillers: two good for `Sense1`, two good for `Sense2`, two bad, each pair with contrasting frequencies. The MONOSEMOUS verbs in our dataset have a total of four patient-fillers: two good and two bad, each pair with contrasting frequencies. This dataset constitutes the first thematic fit judgement dataset that systematically manipulates polysemy and frequency.

We found that human judgements of thematic fit are affected by the number of senses that a verb has (good role-fillers for MONOSEMOUS verbs are judged better than those for POLYSEMOUS verbs, and bad role-fillers are judged worse for MONOSEMOUS verbs than for POLYSEMOUS verbs), and that this effect cannot be explained away by the verb's frequency. This effect may reflect the different levels of constraint that a MONOSEMOUS vs. POLYSEMOUS verb exerts on its arguments. A further important finding was that the frequency of a role-filler has little influence on thematic fit judgements. This supports the notion that semantic similarity and thematic fit are extremely important notions for modeling thematic fit well.

We then evaluated distributional memory models and computational estimation methods on this dataset, comparing methods that can account for verb polysemy by clustering most typical fillers (*kClusters*) to methods that assume a single verb sense (*Centroid*). Our results show that the method that allows for representing verb polysemy consistently outperforms the traditional single-centroid method by Baroni and Lenci (2010). As expected, the most substantial improvements are achieved for POLYSEMOUS verbs, but we also found that model performance on MONOSEMOUS verbs was not hurt by using the *kClusters* method.

The data we collected also suggests that both the probability of the verb sense and the similarity of a role-filler to a prototypical argument for a specific verb sense play a role in human thematic fit judgements: this explains why highly prototypical role fillers for MONOSEMOUS verbs get significantly higher thematic fit judgements than highly prototypical role-fillers for the most frequent verb sense of a POLYSEMOUS verb, and why, in turn, highly prototypical role-fillers for a less frequent verb sense get again significantly lower thematic fit judgements in comparison.

A model implementing this would conceptually estimate thematic fit in terms of a noun's surprisal given the verb ($-\log P(\mathit{filler}|\mathit{verb})$), thereby using the semantic vector space as a back-off model in order to handle rare or unseen combinations of verbs and their arguments. The importance of this is highlighted by our result that noun frequency had little effect on thematic fit judgements. In all, polysemy, frequency, and thematic fit are intertwined in a complex web of dependencies, but the more carefully we obtain human judgements, the more equipped we are to build highly accurate computational models.

Acknowledgments

This research was funded by the German Research Foundation (DFG) as part of SFB 1102: "Information Density and Linguistic Encoding." Also, the authors wish to thank the four anonymous reviewers whose valuable ideas contributed to this paper.

References

Baroni, M. and Lenci, A. (2010). Distributional memory: A general framework for corpus-based semantics. *Computational Linguistics*, 36(4):673–721.

Binder, K. S., Duffy, S. A., and Rayner, K. (2001). The effects of thematic fit and discourse context on syntactic ambiguity resolution. *Journal of Memory and Language*, 44(2):297–324.

Bird, S., Klein, E., and Loper, E. (2009). *Natural Language Processing with Python*. O'Reilly Media.

Caliński, T. and Harabasz, J. (1974). A dendrite method for cluster analysis. *Communications in Statistics—Simulation and Computation*, 3(1):1–27.

Collobert, R. and Weston, J. (2007). Fast semantic extraction using a novel neural network architecture. In *Annual Meeting—Association for Computational Linguistics*, volume 45, page 560.

Collobert, R., Weston, J., Bottou, L., Karlen, M., Kavukcuoglu, K., and Kuksa, P. (2011). Natural language processing (almost) from scratch. *The Journal of Machine Learning Research*, 12:2493–2537.

Davies, M. (2008). The corpus of contemporary american english (COCA): 400+ million words, 1990-present. Available online at `http://www.americancorpus.org`.

Ehrlich, S. F. and Rayner, K. (1981). Contextual effects on word perception and eye movements during reading. *Journal of verbal learning and verbal behavior*, 20(6):641–655.

Erk, K. (2012). Vector space models of word meaning and phrase meaning: A survey. *Language and Linguistics Compass*, 6(10):635–653.

Erk, K., Padó, S., and Padó, U. (2010). A flexible, corpus-driven model of regular and inverse selectional preferences. *Computational Linguistics*, 36(4):723–763.

Fellbaum, C. (1998). *WordNet: an electronic lexical database*. Wiley Online Library.

Greenberg, C., Sayeed, A., and Demberg, V. (2015). Improving unsupervised vector-space thematic fit evaluation via role-filler prototype clustering. In *Proceedings of the 2015 conference of the North American chapter of the Association for Computational Linguistics – Human Language Technologies*, Denver, USA.

Long, J. S. and Ervin, L. H. (2000). Using heteroscedasticity consistent standard errors in the linear regression model. *The American Statistician*, 54(3):217–224.

McRae, K., Spivey-Knowlton, M. J., and Tanenhaus, M. K. (1998). Modeling the influence of thematic fit (and other constraints) in on-line sentence comprehension. *Journal of Memory and Language*, 38(3):283–312.

Nivre, J., Hall, J., Nilsson, J., Chanev, A., Eryigit, G., Kübler, S., Marinov, S., and Marsi, E. (2007). MaltParser: A language-independent system for data-driven dependency parsing. *Natural Language Engineering*, 13(2):95–135.

Padó, U. (2007). *The integration of syntax and semantic plausibility in a wide-coverage model of human sentence processing*. PhD thesis, Saarland University.

Padó, U., Crocker, M. W., and Keller, F. (2009). A probabilistic model of semantic plausibility in sentence processing. *Cognitive Science*, 33(5):794–838.

Resnik, P. (1996). Selectional constraints: An information-theoretic model and its computational realization. *Cognition*, 61(1):127–159.

Sayeed, A. and Demberg, V. (2014). Combining unsupervised syntactic and semantic models of thematic fit. In *Proceedings of the first Italian Conference on Computational Linguistics (CLiC-it 2014)*.

Vandekerckhove, B., Sandra, D., and Daelemans, W. (2009). A robust and extensible exemplar-based model of thematic fit. In *EACL 2009, 12th Conference of the European Chapter of the Association for Computational Linguistics, Proceedings of the Conference, Athens, Greece, March 30 - April 3, 2009*, pages 826–834.

An Evaluation and Comparison of Linguistic Alignment Measures

Yang Xu and **David Reitter**
College of Information Science and Technologies
The Pennsylvania State University
University Park, PA 16802, USA
yang.xu@psu.edu, reitter@psu.edu

Abstract

Linguistic alignment has emerged as an important property of conversational language and a driver of mutual understanding in dialogue. While various computational measures of linguistic alignment in corpus and experimental data have been devised, a systematic evaluation of them is missing. In this study, we first evaluate the sensitivity and distributional properties of three measures, indiscriminate local linguistic alignment (LLA), Spearman's correlation coefficient (SCC), and repetition decay (RepDecay). Then we apply them in a study of interactive alignment and individual differences to see how well they conform to the Interactive Alignment Model (IAM), and how well they can reveal the individual differences in alignment propensity. Our results suggest that LLA has the overall best performance.

1 Introduction

The alignment of language between dialogue partners has garnered much interest in the computational linguistics community. Alignment not only provides insight into the mechanisms of dialogue, but also has the potential to improve both human-computer dialogue systems and the analysis tool-chain. In this context, alignment refers to the convergence of linguistic choices among interlocutors. This may happen at different representational levels, such as the phonological, lexical and syntactic (Garrod and Anderson, 1987). Alignment, also known as entrainment or accommodation, has become recognized as a key feature of linguistic communication.

Several theoretical accounts exist that address the nature and implications of linguistic alignment. In psycholinguistics, the Interactive Alignment Model (IAM) assumes that interlocutors align their linguistic representations (Pickering and Garrod, 2004), from lower ones (lexical, syntactic) to higher ones (e.g., semantics), leading to shared situation models. Sociolinguistic studies point out that interactants converge in their communication styles to signal social affinity and diverge to emphasize social distance (Danescu-Niculescu-Mizil and Lee, 2011; Giles, 2008). Furthermore, evidence has been found showing that certain individuals tend to have higher propensity of alignment than others (Gnisci, 2005; E. Jones et al., 1999; S. Jones et al., 2014; Willemyns et al., 1997).

Several computational measures have been developed to help validating these theoretical accounts. Some of them use the probability of co-occurrence of words (or other linguistic elements) to describe the language alignment (Church, 2000; Dubey, Sturt, and Keller, 2005; Reitter, Keller, and Moore, 2006), while some others take inspiration from documents similarity measures (Huffaker et al., 2006; S. Jones et al., 2014; Wang, Reitter, and Yen, 2014).

However, little research is available that evaluates the properties of these linguistic alignment measures. How sensitive are these measures? What kind of distributions do they have? Can they consistently describe the alignment at multiple linguistic levels (e.g., lexical and syntactic)? Can they describe the individual differences in propensity of alignment? Essentially, are they good/reliable measures? These questions are not answered (or fully answered) yet.

Proceedings of CMCL 2015, pages 58–67,

To answer these questions in this study, we first conduct an evaluation of the intrinsic properties of three well defined and commonly used measures, indiscriminate local linguistic alignment (LLA) (Fusaroli et al., 2012; Wang, Reitter, and Yen, 2014), Spearman's correlation coefficient (SCC) (Huffaker et al., 2006; Kilgarriff, 2001), and repetition decay (RepDecay) (Reitter, Keller, and Moore, 2006), in which two basic properties are investigated, normality of distribution and sensitivity. Then we apply these measures to a study about the IAM and individual differences in alignment propensity as an extrinsic evaluation. We examine how well they follow the basic assumption of IAM, i.e., showing correlations between alignment at lexical and syntactic levels, and how well they can reveal the individual differences in alignment propensity.

Our study aims to provide potential guidance to future studies of linguistic alignment in terms of which computational measures to use. Basically, we favor a measure that has good normality in its distribution, that has higher sensitivity, and that conforms with the IAM theory and the existing findings about individual differences in alignment propensity.

2 Related Work

We will first briefly review the existing computational measures of linguistic alignment. Then we give a short reivew of IAM and the work on individuals' propensity of alignment.

2.1 Existing measures and their limitations

We categorize the existing computational measures into three basic types based on the different methods they use. Though different methods are used, all the three types of measures are conducted upon a similar structure: ($prime$, $target$) pairs, in which $prime$ and $target$ are pieces of text.

Probabilistic measures

Probabilistic measures work on multiple ($prime$, $target$) pairs, and compute the probability of a single word or syntactic rule appearing in $target$ after its appearance in $prime$, by counting the frequency of their co-occurrence. For example, Church (2000) used the first half of documents as $prime$ and the second half as $target$ to measure the lexical adaptation in text. Dubey, Sturt, and Keller (2005) used similar measures to investigate the parallelism effect of syntactic structures in coordinate constructs in corpora. Gries (2005) was among the first to use logistic regression to estimate linear models of syntactic priming.

The limitation of the frequency-based measure is that it needs a relatively large amount of text to conduct the computation, because it uses the observed frequency of words (or syntactic rules), to estimate the probability of co-occurrence.

Document similarity measures

Several measures originate from information retrieval (IR). They have seen little use by corpus-based priming and alignment researchers, although they could conceivably be adopted for our purposes. Huffaker et al. (2006) compared the performance of three computational measures of document similarity in measuring the language convergence in an online community over time. The measures they examined are: Spearman's correlation coefficient (SCC), which measures document similarity based on word frequency and co-occurrence, Zipping, a data compression algorithm that has been used in document comparison, and Latent Semantic Analysis (LSA), a technology for measuring semantic similarity between documents.

Fusaroli et al. (2012) proposed a measure based on probabilities that falls in this category as well: the concept of indiscrimiate local linguistic alignment (LLA). Based on this work, Wang, Reitter, and Yen (2014) implemented LLA at lexical level (LILLA) and syntactic level (SILLA). They essentially measure the number of words (or syntactic rules) that appear in both $prime$ and $target$, normalized by the size of the two text sets.

Repetition decay

Repetition effects have been observed to be short-lived in experiments (e.g., Branigan, Pickering, and Cleland, 1999). Reitter, Keller, and Moore (2006) proposed to use the decay rate of repetition probabilities of syntactic rules to measure the strength of syntactic alignment, and to apply it to all syntactic rules in an observational study.

In their work, Reitter, Keller, and Moore (2006) built a generalized linear model, using the repetition of the syntactic rules as the dependent variable and the distance between $prime$ and $target$ as the predictor. They observed that repetition rate of syntactic rules decays as the distance increases, and used the regression coefficient of the predictor to estimate the strength of syntactic alignment.

Repetition decay gives a strict mathematical account to the alignment phenomena from the probabilistic point of view, and distinguishes the alignment caused by priming from other random repetitions of linguistic elements. One limitation of the repetition decay measure is that it cannot quantify the alignment between a single pair of texts (in fact, it assumes that the simple repetition between two text sets tells us nothing about the overall alignment level). Another limitation is that the fitting a generalized linear model is not as computationally efficient as other measures.

2.2 Interactive alignment model

Pickering and Garrod (2004) proposed the Interactive Alignment Model (IAM) to account for the mechanism that underlie language processing in dialogue. The central assumption of IAM is that, in a dialogue, the linguistic representations employed by the interlocutors become aligned at many levels, and the aligned representations at one level lead to aligned representations at other levels (Pickering and Garrod, 2004). The correlation between different linguistic levels has been shown by corpora-based studies (Wang, Reitter, and Yen, 2014).

2.3 Propensity of alignment

One area that has long been overlooked is the individual speaker's inherent propensity of alignment, i.e., whether some individuals inherently have a stronger tendency to align to their interlocutors than others. Previous studies have shown that individuals in lower social power status tend to converge their language style to those in higher social power status during conversations, e.g., interviewees converging towards their interviewers during employment interviews (Willemyns et al., 1997), students adapting their language to teachers (E. Jones et al., 1999), and witnesses accommodating their linguistic style to that of the lawyers and the judges (Gnisci, 2005). More recently, S. Jones et al. (2014) proposed *Zelig Quotient*, a measure that characterizes an individual's inherent tendency to accommodate to the linguistic style of others, defined by the movement in a high-dimensional linguistic style space. These studies provide evidence that different individuals have different levels of alignment propensity, and this difference can be quantified by computational measures.

However, the main limitation of existing studies is that the individuals' propensity of alignment is only characterized using a proportion of lexical elements. For example, Zelig Quotient only uses functional words (S. Jones et al., 2014). Thus they do not characterize the propensity of alignment at the full range of lexical and syntactic levels.

3 Evaluation Criteria

In this study, we first evaluate two intrinsic properties of the computational measures, and then evaluate their performance in two extrinsic investigations related with IAM and individuals' propensity of alignment.

3.1 Intrinsic evaluation

The two intrinsic properties that we find desirable are: normality of distribution and sensitivity. We expect a good measure to have a normal (or nearly normal) distribution over the whole population, because normal distribution is the most common distribution in nature, and it is desirable from a statistical point of view to have a normal distribution. The sensitivity criterion is straight-forward: we expect a good measure to have satisfactory "resolution", i.e., the capability of detecting relatively small amount of linguistic alignment.

3.2 Extrinsic evaluation

According to the IAM, linguistic alignment between interlocutors occurs at many levels, and aligned representations at one level leads to aligned representations at other levels. For instance, syntactic alignment is enhanced when there are more shared lexical items (Pickering and Garrod, 2004). Thus, it is reasonable to expect that a good measure can capture this effect, demonstrating that higher lexical alignment should co-occur with higher syntactic alignment.

Secondly, due to the empirical evidence that demonstrates the individual's inherent propensity of alignment (Gnisci, 2005; E. Jones et al., 1999; S. Jones et al., 2014; Willemyns et al., 1997), it is reasonable to expect that a good measure of linguistic alignment should be able to characterize an individual's propensity of alignment. If we view the propensity of alignment as a relatively stable individual characteristic that is associated with other social and psychological factors, a good measure should be able to show more variation when measuring text produced by different individuals, and show less variation when measuring text produced by the same individual.

In sum, for the evaluation of the measures' intrinsic properties, we have two criteria: the *normality* of distribution and the *sensitivity*. For the extrinsic evaluation, we examine the performance of measures in three aspects: *consistency*, the measures at lexical level should be correlated with the measures at syntactic level. *Between-individual difference*, whether the measure can reveal significant differences in alignment propensity among different individuals. *Within-individual stability*, whether the alignment measures from the same individual have relatively small variance.

4 Methods

4.1 Processing of corpora

Four corpora are used in this study, including the text data from two online forums, the Cancer Survivors' Network (CSN) [1] and a massive open online course on visual art Art taught on Coursera by Penn State (MOOC), and two published corpora, the Switchboard Corpus (SWBD) (Marcus et al., 1994) and the spoken part of British National Corpus (BNC, 2007).[2]

The threads in CSN and MOOC have similar structures. They consist of an original post followed by reply posts ordered by time. We use a sequence of posts to represent a thread of length n, $[P_0, P_1, P_2, ..., P_n]$, in which P_0 represents the original post started by a forum user, and $P_i (i = 1, ..., n)$ represent the reply posts from other users or the original poster. There is a "reply" relationship between the posts in a thread, indicating that one post is a response to another. For example, if post j (by user B) is a "reply" to post i (by user A), then it means that post j is the direct response from user B to user A in terms of the content of post i. We construct the $(prime,\ target)$ pairs for the linguistic alignment measures based on the "reply" relationship between the posts, i.e., using the original post as $prime$, and the corresponding reply post as $target$. Those pairs of posts whose authors are the same user ("self-reply") are excluded.

Switchboard has only two interlocutors in each conversation, whose utterances are ordered by turn. In BNC, one conversation might contain more than two interlocutors, which results in the relative loose structure of the conversation. The ways we construct $(prime,\ target)$ pairs for the two corpora are similar: selecting one utterance as $prime$, and all the following utterances (within the distance of 10 utterances) that are from the other speaker are selected as $target$ respectively. We restrict the distance to 10 to avoid overtly long conversations. In total, we use all the 80,000 utterances in SWBD and randomly sample 95,441 conversations from BNC.

4.2 LLA

We use the methods implemented by Wang, Reitter, and Yen (2014) to compute the indiscriminate local linguistic alignment (LLA). The lexical and syntactic versions of LLA are implemented and abbreviated as LILLA and SILLA respectively. LILLA and SILLA are the normalized measures of the number of words (or syntactic rules) that occur in both the prime text and the target text:

$$\text{LLA}(P, T) = \frac{\sum_{w_i \in P} \delta(w_i, T)}{length(P) * length(T)} \quad (1)$$

$$\delta(w_i, P) = \begin{cases} 1, \text{if } w_i \in P \\ 0, \text{otherwise} \end{cases} \quad (2)$$

For the computation of LILLA, $|P|$ and $|T|$ are the numbers of words in $prime$ and $target$, and w_i is the individual word in $prime$ (or $target$). For the computation of SILLA, we first use the Stanford Parser (De Marneffe, MacCartney, Manning, et al., 2006) to parse each sentence in $prime$ and $target$ to get their full syntax trees, and then collect all the sub-trees from each sentence. For example, if the first sentence in $prime$ is "I am a teacher.", then the

[1] http://csn.cancer.org

[2] CSN has more than 48,000 threads collected in over 10 years. Switchboard contains more than 80,0000 transcribed utterances annotated with phrase structure trees (Marcus et al., 1994). We use 200 randomly sampled, spontaneous, multi-party conversations from BNC.

parser generates the full syntax tree: (S (NP (PRP I)) (VP (VBP am) (NP (DT a) (NN teacher)))). The sub-trees extracted are: "S $\rightarrow$ NP + VP", "NP $\rightarrow$ PRP", "VP $\rightarrow$ VBP + NP", "NP $\rightarrow$ DT + NN". Then we use the collection of all the sub syntax trees from $prime$ and $target$ as the $|P|$ and $|T|$ in Equation 1, and let w_i refer to the individual syntactic rules.

Differing from Wang, Reitter, and Yen (2014)'s work, we use the natural logarithm of LILLA and SILLA instead, i.e., log-LILLA and log-SILLA, as a simple way to achieve normality of errors.

4.3 Spearman's correlation coefficient

Spearman's correlation coefficient (SCC) originate from the Spearman rank correlation that has been widely used in statistics. It is essentially a non-parametric version of Pearson's correlation coefficient (Myers, Well, and Lorch, 2010). SCC was first proposed by Kilgarriff (2001) to measure the similarity between text and further evaluated by Huffaker et al. (2006). Huffaker et al. (2006) implemented SCC as the following: given a document pair ($prime$, $target$), for each document, rank the n common words in $prime$ and $target$ by frequency. For each word, let d be the difference of ranks in two documents. SCC is defined as the normalized sum of squared differences:

$$\text{SCC} = 1 - \frac{6 \sum d^2}{n(n^2 - 1)} \qquad (3)$$

SCC was originally implemented only for measuring the similarity at lexical level. In this study, we also implement the syntactic version of SCC by applying equation (3) to syntactic rules instead of words, i.e., first parse the $prime$ and $target$ into syntactic rules and get a list of common rules between the two sets, and then compute d in a similar way. In this study, we name the syntactic version of SCC as SCC_{syn}, and the original lexical version as SCC_{lex}.

4.4 Repetition decay

We compute the repetition decay (RepDecay) measure based on the procedure proposed by Reitter, Keller, and Moore (2006). We go through the sequence of ($prime$, $target$) pairs constructed from the corpora with a window of fixed width, e.g., 10 posts/utterances, and look at every element (a word or a syntactic rule) that is in $target$. If one element is also in $prime$, we record this in the variable Rep as 1, and otherwise, we record Rep as 0. Meanwhile, each Rep is associated with another variable $Dist$, which records the distance (from 1 to 10) between $prime$ and $target$. Finally, we build a generalized linear regression model using Rep as the response variable and $ln(Dist)$ as the predictor. We use the regression coefficient β associated with $ln(Dist)$ to represent the strength of linguistic alignment. Theoretically, β is always negative, and the smaller β indicates stronger alignment.

The computation of RepDecay relies on the precise definition of distance between $prime$ and $target$, because its basic assumption is that the priming effect from $prime$ to $target$ decreases as the distance between them increases. In the context of conversations in online forums, the distance between $prime$ and $target$ is difficult to define, because a long distance between two posts, whether it is calculated by time or by number of posts between them, does not necessarily result in the weak priming effect. Based on these considerations, we only compute RepDecay in the SWBD corpus, which solely consists of two-party dialogues. BNC corpus is also excluded because it contains multi-party dialogues that makes it difficult to extract a clear $prime$-$target$ relationship.

4.5 Propensity of alignment

We use all the posts/utterances produced by one individual to measure his/her propensity of alignment. For LLA and SCC, we use all of the ($prime$, $target$) pairs within a certain distance where individual I_i produces the $target$ to represent I_i's propensity of alignment. For RepDecay, we compute the regression coefficient β_i from the sequence of ($prime$, $target$) pairs in which $target$ is produced by I_i and use β_i to represent I_i's propensity of alignment.

We select only those active individuals from the four corpora whose number of posts/utterances is above a common threshold (above 90% of the population). For CSN corpus, we select 1066 active users who have composed at least 50 posts. For MOOC corpus, we select 829 active users who have composed at least 10 posts. For SWBD corpus, all 1296 speakers are selected. For BNC corpus, 502 active speakers who have at least over 26 utterances are se-

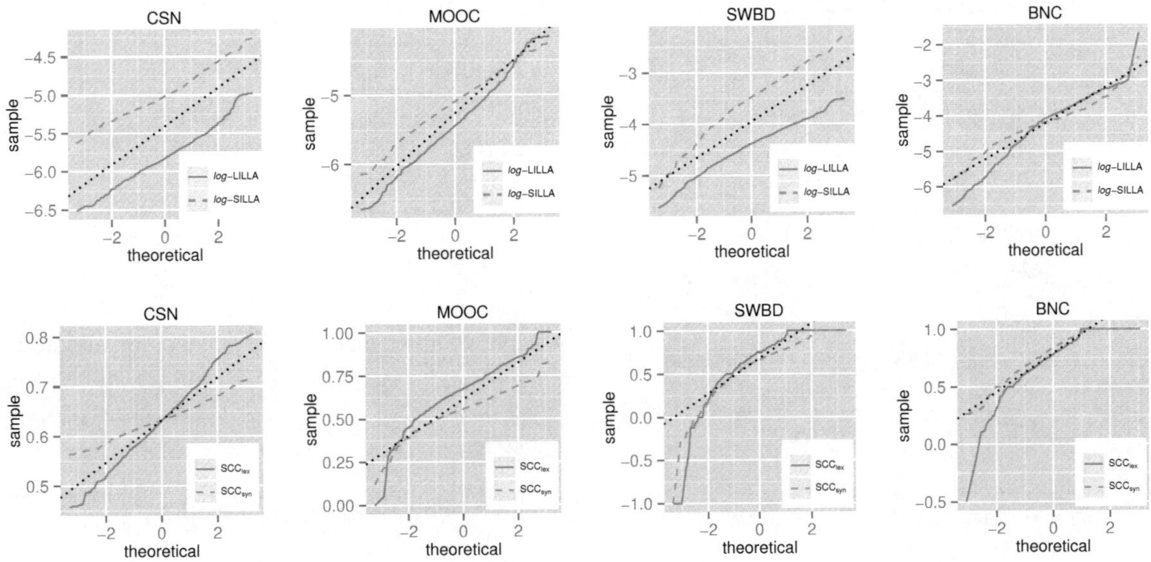

Figure 1: The quantile-quantile plots of LLA and SCC

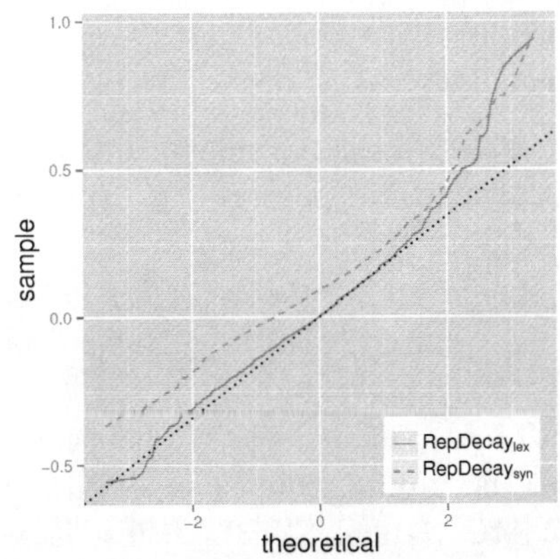

Figure 2: The quantile-quantile plot of RepDecay in SWBD

lected. These active forum-users or speakers are referred to as active individuals.

5 Intrinsic Evaluation Results

5.1 Normality of distribution

We use Shapiro-Wilt test (Shapiro and Wilk, 1965) to examine the normality of distributions of LLA and SCC in all of the four corpora, and the normality of distribution of RepDecay in the SWBD corpus (because RepDecay is only computed in SWBD). The test results show that all these distributions are significantly different from a normal distribution ($p < 0.001$).

But we can still use the quantile-quantile plot of each distribution to compare their normality relatively. Figure 1 show quantile-quantile plots of LLA and SCC in all of the four corpora, and Figure 2 shows the quantile-quantile plot of RepDecay in the SWBD corpus. It can be seen that the quantile-quantile plots of LLA and RepDecay are closer to straight lines (demonstrated by the dot-line) than SCC, thus they have relatively better normality in their distributions.

5.2 Sensitivity

We use NPS Chat Corpus (Forsyth and Martell, 2007) to construct several pieces of pseudo text with different levels of alignment strength, and then investigate the performance of the measures in revealing the difference.

The structure of the pseudo text assembles a sequence of turn-by-turn utterances in a dialogue. We control the strength of alignment by adjusting the probability of a word appearing in an utterance given whether it has appeared in the previous utterance or not. In a non-alignment control condition, the probability of the occurrence of a word is independent of

Table 2: Correlation coefficients between lexical and syntactic measures.

Measure	CSN	MOOC	SWBD	BNC
log-LILLA and *log*-SILLA	0.374***	0.237***	0.188***	0.369***
SCC_{lex} and SCC_{syn}	0.045***	-0.008	-0.001	0.200***
$RepDecay_{lex}$ and $RepDecay_{syn}$	NA	NA	0.695***	NA

$^{*}p < 0.05$, $^{***}p < 0.001$

Table 1: t-test results of comparing measures between different α values

$\alpha = 1$	t-score	
vs.	*log*-LILLA	SCC_{lex}
$\alpha = 1.05$	-1.610	0.000
$\alpha = 1.10$	-2.704*	-0.061
$\alpha = 1.15$	-3.925**	-0.152
$\alpha = 2.25$	-17.47***	-2.463*
...	...	...
$\alpha = 3.00$	-22.23***	-2.839*

$^{*}p < 0.05$, $^{**}p < .01$, $^{***}p < .001$

its occurrence in the previous utterance. In conditions where alignment exists, this probability is dependent on the word's previous occurrences. For example, the prior probability of word "like" is 0.005, if it appears in the first utterance, then we set its probability to appear again in the second utterance is $0.005 * \alpha$ ($\alpha >= 1$), which is slightly larger than the prior. Larger α indicates higher strength of alignment between utterances, and $\alpha = 1$ indicates no alignment.

We use $\alpha = 1, 1.05, 1.1, ..., 3$, to construct sequences of text. Each sequence has 100 utterances, and each utterance randomly has 50 to 100 words. In each sequence, we compute the *log*-LILLA and SCC_{lex} measures for all the 99 pairs of adjacent pairs of utterances, i.e., *u1* and *u2*, *u2* and *u3* etc., using the precedent utterance as $prime$ and the following one as $target$. Finally we conduct pairwise t-test on the measures between the condition of $\alpha = 1$ and the conditions of other α values respectively (Table 1). RepDecay is not included in this analysis, because the decay effect is not considered when we construct the pseudo text.

Table 1 shows that LLA can detect the alignment effect at $\alpha = 1.10$ (at $p < 0.05$), while SCC can only detect $\alpha >= 2.25$. Thus, LLA has higher sensitivity than SCC.

6 Extrinsic Evaluation Results

As introduced in Section 3, we evaluate the performance of LLA, SSC, and RepDecay in three aspects: Consistency across different linguistic representation levels, between-individual difference, and within-individual stability.

6.1 Consistency

We calculate the Pearson correlation coefficients between lexical syntactic measures for LLA, SCC, and RepDecay (Table 2).

It is shown that the correlation between $RepDecay_{lex}$ and $RepDecay_{syn}$ is strongest, followed by the correlation between *log*-LILLA and *log*-SILLA. The correlation between SCC_{lex} and SCC_{syn} is only significant in CSN and BNC, but not in MOOC and SWBD. Thus, it indicates that RepDecay and LLA show better consistency between lexical and syntactic alignment than SCC.

6.2 Between-individual differences

We use one-way ANOVA to examine whether the between-individual differences of alignment propensity outweigh within-individual variance (Table 3). RepDecay is not included in the analysis because it generates only one value for each individual.

While all F scores indicate significant differences, LLA shows higher F scores than SCC. This result indicates that the alignment measures from some individuals are significantly higher than the others, and this tendency holds for both lexical alignment and syntactic alignment.

Table 3: F scores resulting from one-way ANOVAs (All values are significant at $p < 0.001$ level)

Measure	CSN	MOOC	SWBD	BNC
log-LILLA	15.05	2.761	51.52	14.32
log-SILLA	20.66	2.402	25.44	5.289
SCC_{lex}	8.884	1.205	3.448	1.937
SCC_{syn}	1.494	1.185	4.242	3.492

6.3 Within-individual stability

We use the coefficient of variation (CV) (Abdi, 2010) (also known as relative standard deviation), to evaluate the within-individual stability of the measures. CV is defined as the ratio of the standard deviation σ to the mean μ: $c_v = \sigma/\mu$. A smaller CV indicates less variability of a random variable in relation to its mean.

We calculate the CVs of LLA and SCC for each active individual in the four corpora, and then use t-tests to compare LLA vs. SCC (for lexical and syntactic measures respectively). RepDecay is not included in this analysis because it generates one value for each individual and thus there is no within-individual variance.

The t-tests results indicate that log-LILLA has smaller CVs than SCC_{lex} across the four corpora ($p < 0.001$). log-SILLA also has smaller CVs than SCC_{syn} for CSN, MOOC and SWBD corpora ($p < 0.001$), and there is no significant difference for BNC corpus ($p = 0.299$). This indicates that LLA has better within-individual stability than SCC.

7 Conclusions and Discussion

In this study, we evaluate the intrinsic properties of three computational measures of linguistic alignment: indiscriminate local linguistic alignment (LLA), Spearman's correlation coefficient (SCC), and repetition decay (RepDecay). We also evaluate their performance when applied to an extrinsic study about the IAM theory and individuals' alignment propensity.

From the intrinsic evaluations, we find that LLA and RepDecay are more normally distributed than SCC, and that LLA is more sensitivity than SCC. The main cause for the poorer normality of SCC roots in its way of computation: there has to be at least two common elements in order to get a valid value, but if $target$ is a pure repetition of $prime$, the value is always 1. Thus for short utterances that are common in spoken dialogues (SWBD and BNC), they are more likely to generate 1s, which result in the skewed distribution of SCC.

From the extrinsic evaluations, our main conclusions are: First, in terms of the propensity of alignment, both LLA and SCC can reveal significant individual differences. Meanwhile, LLA shows larger effect size for individual differences, and higher within-individual stability than SCC. Second, in terms of the correlation between alignment at the lexical and syntactic levels, RepDecay shows the strongest correlation, but LLA also consistently shows strong correlation across all corpora investigated. However, SCC does not consistently show this correlation.

Our study provides potential suggestions to future computational investigations about linguistic alignment. LLA is more favorable if the research question relates to individuals' inherent propensity of alignment, because it yields more significant between-individual differences and has better within-individual stability. LLA has better normality and sensitivity properties. RepDecay is more favorable if the research question is to explore the correlations between alignment at different linguistic levels, because it shows strongest correlation between lexical and syntactic levels in this study.

For future work, to explore the application of computational measures in revealing individuals' propensity of alignment at multiple linguistic levels (other than lexical and syntactic) could be an interesting direction.

Acknowledgments

We would like to thank the American Cancer Society (Kenneth Portier and Greta E. Greer) for curating and providing the Cancer Survivor Network corpus, and Anna Divinksy and Bart Pursel for the Art MOOC corpus. We thank John Yen and Yafei Wang for their helpful discussions.

References

Abdi, Hervé (2010). "Coefficient of variation". In: *Encyclopedia of Research Design. SAGE, Thousand Oaks, CA*, pp. 169–171.

BNC (2007). *The British National Corpus, version 3 (BNC XML Edition)*. URL: http://www.natcorp.ox.ac.uk/.

Branigan, Holly P., Martin J. Pickering, and Alexandra A. Cleland (1999). "Syntactic priming in language production: Evidence for rapid decay". In: *Psychonomic Bulletin and Review* 6.4, pp. 635–640.

Church, Kenneth W (2000). "Empirical estimates of adaptation: the chance of two noriegas is closer to p/2 than p 2". In: *Proceedings of the 18th Conference on Computational linguistics-Volume 1*. Association for Computational Linguistics, pp. 180–186.

Danescu-Niculescu-Mizil, Cristian and Lillian Lee (2011). "Chameleons in imagined conversations: A new approach to understanding coordination of linguistic style in dialogs". In: *Proceedings of the 2nd Workshop on Cognitive Modeling and Computational Linguistics*. Association for Computational Linguistics, pp. 76–87.

De Marneffe, Marie-Catherine, Bill MacCartney, Christopher D Manning, et al. (2006). "Generating typed dependency parses from phrase structure parses". In: *Proceedings of LREC*. Vol. 6, pp. 449–454.

Dubey, Amit, Patrick Sturt, and Frank Keller (2005). "Parallelism in coordination as an instance of syntactic priming: Evidence from corpus-based modeling". In: *Proceedings of the Conference on Human Language Technology and Empirical Methods in Natural Language Processing*. Association for Computational Linguistics, pp. 827–834.

Forsyth, Eric N and Craig H Martell (2007). "Lexical and discourse analysis of online chat dialog". In: *Semantic Computing, 2007. ICSC 2007. International Conference on*. IEEE, pp. 19–26.

Fusaroli, Riccardo et al. (2012). "Coming to terms quantifying the benefits of linguistic coordination". In: *Psychological Science* 8, pp. 931–939.

Garrod, Simon and Anthony Anderson (1987). "Saying what you mean in dialogue: A study in conceptual and semantic co-ordination". In: *Cognition* 27.2, pp. 181–218.

Giles, Howard (2008). *Communication accommodation theory*. Sage.

Gnisci, Augusto (2005). "Sequential strategies of accommodation: A new method in courtroom". In: *British Journal of Social Psychology* 44.4, pp. 621–643.

Gries, Stefan Th. (2005). "Syntactic priming: A corpus-based approach". In: *Journal of Psycholinguistic Research* 34.4, pp. 365–399.

Huffaker, David et al. (2006). "Computational measures for language similarity across time in online communities". In: *Proceedings of the HLT-NAACL 2006 Workshop on Analyzing Conversations in Text and Speech*. Association for Computational Linguistics, pp. 15–22.

Jones, Elizabeth et al. (1999). "Strategies of accommodation: Development of a coding system for conversational interaction". In: *Journal of Language and Social Psychology* 18.2, pp. 123–151.

Jones, Simon et al. (2014). "Finding Zelig in Text: A Measure for Normalizing Linguistic Accommodation". In: *25th International Conference on Computational Linguistics*. University of Bath.

Kilgarriff, Adam (2001). "Comparing corpora". In: *International journal of corpus linguistics* 6.1, pp. 97–133.

Marcus, Mitchell et al. (1994). "The Penn Treebank: annotating predicate argument structure". In: *Proceedings of the workshop on Human Language Technology*. Association for Computational Linguistics, pp. 114–119.

Myers, Jerome L, Arnold Well, and Robert Frederick Lorch (2010). *Research design and statistical analysis*. Routledge.

Pickering, Martin J. and Simon Garrod (2004). "Toward a mechanistic psychology of dialogue". In: *Behavioral and brain sciences* 27.02, pp. 169–190.

Reitter, David, Frank Keller, and Johanna D Moore (2006). "Computational modelling of structural priming in dialogue". In: *Proceedings of the Human Language Technology Conference of the NAACL*. Association for Computational Linguistics, pp. 121–124.

Shapiro, Samuel Sanford and Martin B Wilk (1965). "An analysis of variance test for normality (complete samples)". In: *Biometrika*, pp. 591–611.
Wang, Yafei, David Reitter, and John Yen (2014). "Linguistic Adaptation in Conversation Threads: Analyzing Alignment in Online Health Communities". In: *Proc. Cognitive Modeling and Computational Linguistics. Workshop at the Mtg. of the Association for Computational Linguistics*.
Willemyns, Michael et al. (1997). "Accent Accommodation in the Job Interview Impact of Interviewer Accent and Gender". In: *Journal of Language and Social Psychology* 16.1, pp. 3–22.

Utility-based evaluation metrics for models of language acquisition: A look at speech segmentation

Lawrence Phillips & Lisa Pearl
University of California, Irvine
3151 Social Sciences Plaza
Irvine, CA 92697 USA
[lawphill, lpearl]@uci.edu

Abstract

Models of language acquisition are typically evaluated against a "gold standard" meant to represent adult linguistic knowledge, such as orthographic words for the task of speech segmentation. Yet adult knowledge is rarely the target knowledge for the stage of acquisition being modeled, making the gold standard an imperfect evaluation metric. To supplement the gold standard evaluation metric, we propose an alternative utility-based metric that measures whether the acquired knowledge facilitates future learning. We take the task of speech segmentation as a case study, assessing previously proposed models of segmentation on their ability to generate output that (i) enables creation of language-specific segmentation cues that rely on stress patterns, and (ii) assists the subsequent acquisition task of learning word meanings. We find that behavior that maximizes gold standard performance does not necessarily maximize the utility of the acquired knowledge, highlighting the benefit of multiple evaluation metrics.

1 The problem with model evaluation

Over the past decades, computational modeling has become an increasingly useful tool for studying the ways children acquire their native language. Modeling allows researchers to explicitly evaluate learning strategies by whether these strategies would enable acquisition success. But how do researchers determine if a particular learning strategy is successful? Traditionally, models have been evaluated against adult linguistic knowledge, typically captured in an explicit "gold standard". If the modeled learner succeeds at acquiring this adult linguistic knowledge, then it is said to have succeeded and the learning strategy is held up as a viable option for how the acquisition process might work.

Gold standard evaluation has two key benefits. First, it provides a uniform measure of evaluation, especially when gold standards are relatively similar across corpora (e.g. orthographic segmentation for speech). Second, this kind of evaluation is typically straightforward to implement for labeled corpora, and so is easy to use for model comparison.

Still, there are several potential disadvantages to gold standard evaluation. First, the choice of an appropriate gold standard is non-trivial for many linguistic tasks since there is disagreement about what the adult knowledge actually is (e.g., speech segmentation, grammatical categorization, syntactic parsing). Second, implementation may require a large amount of time-consuming manual annotation (e.g. visual scene labeling for word-object mapping). Third, and perhaps most importantly, it is unclear that adult knowledge is the appropriate output for some modeled learning strategies, particularly those that are meant to occur early in acquisition.

For example, consider the early stages of speech segmentation that rely only on probabilistic cues. The earliest evidence of speech segmentation comes at six months (Bortfeld, Morgan, Golinkoff, & Rathbun, 2005) and it appears that probabilistic cues to segmentation, which are language-independent because their implementation does not depend on the specific language being acquired, give way to language-dependent cues between eight and nine

Proceedings of CMCL 2015, pages 68–78,
Denver, Colorado, June 4, 2015.

months (Johnson & Jusczyk, 2001; Thiessen & Saffran, 2003). So, accurate models of this early stage of speech segmentation should output the knowledge that a nine-month-old has, and this may differ quite significantly from the knowledge an adult has about how to segment speech.

Unfortunately, addressing this last issue with gold standard evaluation is non-trivial. One strategy might be to create a gold standard representing age-appropriate knowledge. However, without empirical data that can identify exactly what children's knowledge at a particular age is, this is difficult. Because of this, few (if any) age-specific gold standards exist for the many acquisition tasks that we wish to evaluate learning strategies for. An alternative is to compare model results against qualitative patterns that have been reported in the developmental literature. For instance, Lignos (2012) compares his segmentation model results against qualitative patterns of over- and undersegmentation reported in diary data (Brown, 1973; Peters, 1983). Still, such comparisons are often difficult to make since the behavioral data may come from children of different ages than the modeled learners (e.g., the segmentation patterns mentioned above come from two- and three-year-olds while the modeled learners are at most nine months old).

So, the essence of the evaluation problem is this: the true target for model output is potentially unknown, but we still wish to evaluate different models. Fortunately for language acquisition modelers, this is exactly the problem faced in computer science when unsupervised learning algorithms are applied and a gold standard does not exist. There are two main ways a model without a gold standard can be explicitly evaluated (Theodoridis & Koutroubas, 1999; von Luxburg, Williamson, & Guyon, 2011):

1. Apply real-world, expert knowledge to determine if the output is reasonable.

2. Measure the "utility" of the output.

Adding these two evaluation approaches to a language acquisition modeler's toolbox can help alleviate the issues surrounding gold standards. Still, the first option of applying expert knowledge is often time intensive, since this typically involves querying human knowledge. Moreover, given the key concern about what the output of language acquisition models ought to look like anyway, it is unclear that querying linguistic experts is appropriate. Given this, we focus on measuring the utility of the model's output (Mercier, 1912; von Luxburg et al., 2011) to supplement a gold standard analysis.

This means we must be more precise about "utility". Because children acquire linguistic knowledge and then apply that acquired knowledge to learn more of their native language system (Landau & Gleitman, 1985; Morgan & Demuth, 1996), one definition of utility for language acquisition is for the model output to facilitate further knowledge acquisition. Importantly, determining what future knowledge is acquired is often much easier than determining the exact state of that knowledge, as with a gold standard. This is because we often have empirical data about the order in which linguistic knowledge is acquired (e.g., language-independent cues to speech segmentation are used to identify language-dependent cues, which are then used to facilitate further segmentation). We can use these empirical data to identify what a model's output should be used *for*, and assess if the acquired knowledge helps the learner acquire the appropriate additional knowledge. Then, if a modeled strategy yields this kind of useful knowledge, the modeled strategy should be counted as successful; in contrast, if the acquired knowledge isn't useful (or is actively harmful), then this is a mark of failure. Under this view, a strategy's utility is equivalent to its ability to prepare the learner for subsequent acquisition tasks.

As we will see when we apply this utility-based evaluation to speech segmentation strategies, we may still encounter some familiar evaluation issues. In particular, to evaluate whether a model's output prepares a learner for subsequent acquisition tasks, we must have some idea as to what counts as "good enough" preparation for those subsequent tasks. The simplest answer seems to be that "good enough" for the subsequent task means that the output for that task is "good enough" for the next task after that. In some sense then, the best indicator of utility would be that the modeled strategy yields adult level knowledge once the entire acquisition process is complete. However, it is currently impractical to model the entire language acquisition process. Instead, we have to restrict ourselves to smaller segments of the entire process – here, two sequential stages. Given the available empirical data, it may be that we have a better idea about what children's knowledge is for the second stage than we do for the first stage. That is, an age-appropriate gold standard may be available for the subsequent acquisition task. For both utility evaluations we do here, we have something like this for each subsequent task, though it is likely still an imperfect approximation of young children's knowledge.

We note that this utility-based approach differs from a joint inference approach, where two tasks occur simultaneously and information from one task helpfully informs the other (Jones, Johnson, & Frank, 2010; Feldman, Griffiths, Goldwater, & Morgan, 2013; Dillon, Dunbar, & Idsardi, 2013; Doyle & Levy, 2013; Börschinger & Johnson, 2014). Joint inference is appropriate when we have empirical evidence that children accomplish both tasks at the same time. In contrast, the utility-based evaluation approach is appropriate when empirical evidence suggests children accomplish tasks sequentially.

In this paper, we consider the task of speech segmentation and investigate different ways of assessing the utility of previously proposed strategies. Notably, these strategies have generally succeeded when evaluated against some version of a gold standard (Phillips & Pearl, in press, 2014a, 2014b). We first briefly review speech segmentation in infants, and then describe the segmentation strategies previously investigated: a Bayesian segmentation strategy (Goldwater, Griffiths, & Johnson, 2009; Pearl, Goldwater, & Steyvers, 2011) and a subtractive segmentation strategy (Lignos, 2011, 2012). We then evaluate each modeled strategy on two utility measures relating to (i) the creation of language-dependent segmentation cues relying on stress, and (ii) the subsequent acquisition task of learning word meanings.

We find that the strategies differ significantly in their ability to identify stress segmentation cues and facilitate word meaning acquisition, with the Bayesian strategy yielding more useful output than the subtractive segmentation strategy. We discuss how these utility results relate to other qualitative patterns, such as oversegmentation, noting that behavior that maximizes performance against a gold standard does not necessarily maximize the utility of the acquired knowledge for subsequent learning.

2 Speech segmentation strategies

One of the first acquisition tasks infants solve is identifying useful units in fluent speech, and the useful units are typically thought of as words. While word boundaries are inconsistently marked by pauses (Cole & Jakimik, 1980), there are several linguistic cues that infants can leverage (Morgan & Saffran, 1995; Jusczyk, Houston, & Newsome, 1999; Mattys, Jusczyk, & Luce, 1999; Jusczyk, Hohne, & Baumann, 1999; Johnson & Jusczyk, 2001). However, many of these cues are specific to the language being acquired (e.g., whether words of the language generally begin or end with a stressed syllable), and so require infants to identify some words in the language before the language-specific cue can be instantiated. Fortunately, experimental evidence suggests that infants can leverage language-independent probabilistic cues to identify that initial seed pool of words (Saffran, Aslin, & Newport, 1996; Aslin, Saffran, & Newport, 1998; Thiessen & Saffran, 2003; Pelucchi, Hay, & Saffran, 2009). This had led to significant interest in the early probabilistic segmentation strategies infants use (Brent, 1999; Batchelder, 2002; Goldwater et al., 2009; Blanchard, Heinz, & Golinkoff, 2010; Pearl et al., 2011; Lignos, 2011).

The two strategies we examine here, a Bayesian strategy (Goldwater et al., 2009; Pearl et al., 2011; Phillips & Pearl, 2014a, 2014b, in press) and a subtractive segmentation strategy (Lignos, 2011, 2012), have two attractive properties. First, they can be implemented so that the modeled learner perceives the input as a sequence of syllables, in accord with the infant speech perception experimental literature (Jusczyk and Derrah (1987); Bertonicini, Bijeljac-Babic, Jusczyk, Kennedy, and Mehler (1988); Bijeljac-Babic, Bertoncini, and Mehler (1993); Eimas (1999) and see Phillips and Pearl (in press) for more detailed discussion). Second, their syllable-based implementations perform well on English child-directed speech when compared against a gold standard (Phillips & Pearl, in press; Lignos, 2011).

2.1 Bayesian segmentation

The Bayesian strategy[1] has two variants, using either a unigram or bigram generative assumption for how words are generated in fluent speech. The model assumes utterances are produced via a Dirichlet process (Ferguson, 1973). In the unigram case, the identity of the ith word is chosen according to (1):

$$P(w_i|w_1 \dots w_{i-1}) = \frac{n_{i-1}(w) + \alpha P_0(w)}{i - 1 + \alpha} \quad (1)$$

where n_{i-1} is the number of times w appears in the previous $i-1$ words, α is a free parameter, and P_0 is a base distribution specifying the probability that a novel word will consist of the perceptual units $x_1 \dots x_m$ (which are syllables here):

$$P_0(w = x_1 \dots x_m) = \prod_j P(x_j) \quad (2)$$

In the bigram case, the model assumes a hierarchical Dirichlet Process (Teh, Jordan, Beal, & Blei, 2006) and additionally tracks the frequencies of two-word sequences:

$$P(w_i|w_{i-1} = w', w_1 \dots w_{i-2}) = \frac{n_{i-1}(w', w) + \beta P_1(w)}{n(w') - 1 + \beta} \quad (3)$$

$$P_1(w_i = w) = \frac{b_{i-1}(w) + \gamma P_0(w)}{b - 1 + \gamma} \quad (4)$$

where $n_{i-1}(w', w)$ is the number of times the bigram (w', w) has occurred in the first $i-1$ words, $n(w')$ is the number of bigrams beginning with word w', $b_{i-1}(w)$ is the number of times w has occurred as the second word of a bigram, b is the total number of bigrams, and β and γ are free parameters.[2]

In both the unigram and bigram variants, this generative model implicitly incorporates preferences for smaller lexicons by preferring words that appear frequently (due to equations 1, 3, and 4) and preferring shorter words in the lexicon (due to equation 2). These can be thought of as domain-general parsimony biases.

The ideal (**Batch**) learner for this model is taken from Goldwater et al. (2009) and utilizes Gibbs sampling (Geman & Geman, 1984) to batch process the entire input corpus, sampling every potential word boundary 20,000 times. This represents the most idealized learner, since Gibbs sampling is guaranteed to converge on the segmentation which best fits the underlying generative model. Because this learner does not include cognitive processing or memory constraints, we also implement one of the constrained learners developed by Pearl et al. (2011) that better approximates actual human inference. In addition, that constrained learner was shown to be very successful on English (Phillips & Pearl, in press).

The constrained (**Online**) learner processes data incrementally, but uses a Decayed Markov Chain Monte Carlo algorithm (Marthi, Pasula, Russell, & Peres, 2002) to implement a kind of limited short-term memory. This learner is similar to the Batch learner in that it uses something like Gibbs sampling. However, the Online learner does not sample all potential boundaries; instead, it samples s previous boundaries using the decay function b^{-d} to select the boundary to sample, where b is the number of potential boundary locations between the boundary under consideration b_c and the end of the current utterance, while d is the decay rate. Thus, the further b_c is from the end of the current utterance, the less likely it is to be sampled. Larger values of d indicate a stricter memory constraint. All results presented here use a set, non-optimized value for d of 1.5, which was chosen to implement a heavy memory constraint (e.g., 90% of samples come from the current utterance, while 96% are in the current or previous utterance). Having sampled a set of boundaries[3], the learner can then update its beliefs about those boundaries and subsequently update its lexicon before moving on to the next utterance.

[1] Called DPSEG by Goldwater et al. (2009).

[2] α, β, and γ for all modeled learners were chosen, as in previous work, to maximize the gold standard word token F-score of the unigram and bigram Batch learner: $\alpha = 1, \beta = 1, \gamma = 90$.

[3] The Online learner samples $s = 20,000$ boundaries per utterance. For a syllable-based learner, this works out to approximately 74% less processing than the Batch learner (Phillips & Pearl, in press).

2.2 Subtractive segmentation

The subtractive segmentation strategy (Lignos, 2011) processes the corpus one utterance a time. It begins by assuming that every utterance is a single word and then, as it adds vocabulary to its lexicon, it segments out those words when possible. The specific variant we investigate is the beam search subtractive segmenter without stress information, which is allowed the same segmentation cues as the Bayesian strategy.

In cases where there is ambiguity with respect to a particular word boundary, the model considers the two possible segmentations (the one with the boundary and the one without) and chooses the one with the higher score. A segmentation's score is the geometric mean of the score of each word in the potential segmentation. A word's score is determined by two factors: (i) its frequency in previous inferred segmentations, and (ii) how often it has been part of potential segmentation that was previously rejected.

2.3 Baseline comparison: Random oracle

We additionally examine a random oracle baseline (Lignos, 2012). This strategy makes guesses about word boundaries as a series of Bernoulli trials, where the probability of a boundary p_b is set to the true probability according to the gold standard. Although this is unrealistic as an actual strategy infants use because it assumes knowledge of word boundary frequency, this strategy serves as a best-case scenario for what random guessing might achieve.

3 Previous results with the gold standard

These strategies were evaluated against a gold standard in English by using the UCI Brent Syllables corpus of English child-directed speech (Phillips & Pearl, in press) available through CHILDES (MacWhinney, 2000), which contains 28,391 utterances of speech directed to American English children between six and nine months old. Word token F-scores (shown in Table 1) provide a convenient summary statistic for segmentation model evaluation, where the F-score is the harmonic mean of precision and recall. So, the F-score balances how accurate the set of identified words is (precision = $\frac{\#\ correctly\ identified}{\#\ identified}$) with how complete the set of identified words is (recall = $\frac{\#correctly\ identified}{\#\ true}$).

Word Token F-scores			
Batch (Uni)	0.531	Online (Uni)	0.551
Batch (Bi)	0.771	Online (Bi)	0.863
Subtractive Seg	0.879	Random	0.588

Table 1: Word token F-score results on the UCI Brent Syllables corpus as reported by Phillips and Pearl (in press) for the Bayesian learners (Batch vs. Online, Unigram vs. Bigram), the subtractive segmenter, and the random oracle baseline.

Based on this evaluation metric, the subtractive segmenter performs the best, though the Bayesian Online bigram learner does nearly as well. Notably, the Bayesian unigram learners suffer significantly in comparison, doing worse than even the random oracle baseline. This suggests the unigram assumption is harmful if the goal is to generate the adult knowledge represented in the gold standard.

4 Stress cue identification

A language-dependent segmentation cue that infants use fairly early is their native language's predominant stress pattern (Jusczyk, Houston, & Newsome, 1999; Morgan & Saffran, 1995). In particular, while seven-month-olds rely more on probabilistic cues, nine-month-olds rely more on stress-based cues (Johnson & Jusczyk, 2001; Thiessen & Saffran, 2003). So, while probabilistic cues and stress-based cues may be used jointly (Lignos, 2012; Doyle & Levy, 2013), infants likely use probabilistic cues only until enough evidence has been accumulated to identify the language-dependent stress cue. In particular, infants want to identify whether words tend to begin with stressed syllables or end with stressed syllables, since that can provide a convenient heuristic for identifying word boundaries. For example, if words begin with stressed syllables, then a stressed syllable signals that the previous word has ended and a new word has begun.

Given this, a measure of the utility of a segmentation strategy's output is whether the generated lexicon yields the appropriate stress cue. To determine this, we must first identify where stressed syllables are in the English child-directed data. Because the UCI Brent Syllables corpus does not mark stress, we make use of the English Callhome Lexicon (Kingsbury, Strassel, McLemore, & MacIntyre,

1997) to identify the main stress in words. For child-register words not found in standard dictionaries (like *moosha*), we manually coded the stress when the words were familiar enough to us to deduce the stress pattern. If a word was not familiar enough for us to be confident about its stress pattern (e.g., *bonino*), we ignored it for the purposes of this analysis. All words in the analyses presented below were given their dictionary stress patterns. In order to better approximate the stress of actual utterances, monosyllabic words were left unstressed.

Table 2 presents the stress pattern of the bisyllabic word types in each learner's lexicon.[4] Our corpus of English child-directed speech has 1344 unique bisyllabic words with 89.9% beginning with a stressed syllable (SW: *báby*) and 10.1% ending with a stressed syllable (WS: *ballóon*), as shown by the *Adult Seg* row. For the learner to correctly infer that English words tend to be stress-initial, the inferred lexicon should have more words with the stress-initial pattern. This serves as an approximate age-appropriate gold standard, since the goal is to match the qualitative stress distribution pattern that would yield the stress cue English nine-month-olds use (i.e., stressed syllables begin words).

	SW	WS
Adult Seg	**89.9%**	**10.1%**
Batch (Uni)	80.0%	20.0%
Online (Uni)	80.8%	19.2%
Batch (Bi)	80.4%	19.6%
Online (Bi)	79.6%	20.4%
Subtractive Seg	59.4%	40.6%
Random	68.5%	31.5%

Table 2: Stress pattern results for all learners on bisyllabic word types. Percentages are calculated out of all bisyllabic words identified by the model.

All Bayesian learners capture the qualitative stress pattern, and come fairly close to capturing the quantitative distribution, with 79.6% - 80.8% of the bisyllabic word types having word-initial stress (SW). The subtractive segmenter weakly shows the same pattern, identifying more bisyllabic word types with word-initial stress (59.4% SW). The random oracle baseline actually produces a stronger word-initial bias than the subtractive segmenter (68.5% SW). This suggests an advantage for the Bayesian strategy when it comes to inferring the English stress segmentation cue from the bisyllabic words in the inferred lexicon.

[4]We note that we calculate this over word types rather than word tokens, since learners may ignore frequency when deciding how far to extend generalizations (Yang, 2005; Perfors, Ransom, & Navarro, 2014).

When we turn to trisyllabic words, however, the Bayesian strategy no longer does better – both strategies fail to capture the qualitative stress pattern (as does the random oracle baseline). Table 3 shows the results across the 345 trisyllabic word types. The qualitative pattern in the true distribution is similar to the bisyllabic words (though the distribution is less pronounced), with the majority (69.2%) having initial stress. However, all strategies yield a preference for word-medial stress in trisyllabic words (37.4% - 50.1%). Interestingly, if a learner was attempting to infer a segmentation cue, word-medial stress actually doesn't yield an obvious cue – there is no word boundary either immediately before or immediately after the stressed syllable. So, even if the inferred stress pattern is incorrect for trisyllabic words, it may not actually harm a learner who is looking for segmentation cues – it just fails to help.

	SWW	WSW	WWS
Adult Seg	**69.2%**	**2.2%**	**28.6%**
Batch (Uni)	22.7%	50.1%	27.2%
Online (Uni)	22.8%	49.2%	28.0%
Batch (Bi)	22.0%	46.6%	31.4%
Online (Bi)	23.7%	47.7%	28.6%
Subtractive Seg	19.1%	48.7%	32.2%
Random	28.6%	37.4%	34.0%

Table 3: Stress pattern results for all learners on trisyllabic word types. Percentages are calculated out of all trisyllabic words identified by the model.

More generally, these results suggest that the word token F-score is not necessarily correlated with knowledge utility, at least when it comes to inferring language-dependent stress-based cues to segmentation. For instance, the Online Bayesian bigram learner and the subtractive segmenter have similar word token F-scores (0.863 vs. 0.879), but generate quantitatively different predictions for the English stress-based segmentation cue. Similarly, the Bayesian unigram learners have far lower word token F-scores (0.531-0.551), yet yield correct predictions for the English stress cue, based on bisyllabic word types.

If any of these strategies are the ones infants use, then we would predict that infants in the early stages of segmentation have different expectations about the prevalent stress pattern for bisyllabic vs. trisyllabic words in English. This is something that can be verified experimentally. However, we do note that the current analyses leading to this prediction are based on particular assumptions about how accurately infants perceive stress in their input (here, perfectly accurately), and so future analyses should consider other cognitively plausible instantiations of infant stress perception. In addition, while this stress analysis was only applied to English here, it is worthwhile to do so for other languages that vary in how their stress system operates.

5 Word meaning

A task that infants tackle after they are somewhat able to segment the speech stream is learning word meaning. In particular, word meaning learning begins as early as six months (Tincoff & Jusczyk, 1999, 2012; Bergelson & Swingley, 2012), focusing on concrete items in the learner's environment like *apple* and *hand*. So, another test of a segmentation strategy's utility is whether the lexicon it generates facilitates this kind of early word-object mapping.

5.1 A model of early word-object mapping

Drawing on the intuition that early word-object mapping could leverage cross-situational learning, Frank, Goodman, and Tenenbaum (2009) developed a Bayesian learning strategy for early word-object mapping. The modeled learner infers a referential lexicon of word-object mappings based on the utterances spoken and the set of objects visually salient in the environment. In the generative model shown in the plate diagram in Figure 1, the learner assumes there are some objects (O) in the environment, and the speaker intends to refer to some subset of them (I) using words. The speaker draws words from the referential lexicon (L) to refer to those intended objects, with non-referential words also occurring in the utterances with some probability. So, based on a set of situations (S) containing observable utterances comprised of words (W) and sets of visually salient objects (O), the modeled learner can infer the referential lexicon L of word-object mappings as well as the specific intended objects (I).

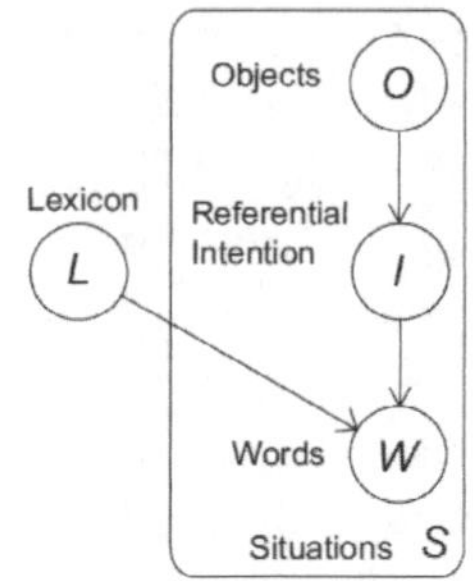

Figure 1: Plate diagram of the Frank et al. (2009) word-object mapping generative model.

This model vastly outperformed other word-object mapping strategies on a sample of English child-directed speech, yielding a referential lexicon that was significantly more accurate (higher precision) compared to other strategies. High lexicon precision is likely more important than high lexical recall for early word-object mapping because this is only the first stage of word meaning learning. So, it is better to have a small set of reliable word-object mappings than a large set of unreliable word-object mappings if the learner is using these mappings to bootstrap future word meaning acquisition.

Notably, the model assumes the utterances are already segmented into words. So, a natural evaluation measure for segmentation strategies is to use the inferred segmentation of the utterances, rather than the adult orthographic segmentation used in the original Frank et al. (2009) demonstration. We can then see if the mapping strategy is still able to identify a reliable referential lexicon. As with the previous utility evaluation, the desired output (a lexicon of word-object mappings) is a gold standard, in this case based on how adults construct word-object mappings. However, because the inferred mappings focus on concrete objects infants are known to learn mappings for, we believe it is at least an approximation of an age-appropriate gold standard.

5.2 Segmentation strategy evaluation

Originally, the word-object model was evaluated on a small subset of 700 utterances from the Rollins corpus from CHILDES (MacWhinney, 2000) which was labeled with visually salient objects (O in the Figure 1). We used this corpus to evaluate the segmentation strategies. We first trained the segmentation strategies on the 28,391 utterances of the UCI Brent Syllables corpus (Phillips & Pearl, in press) so that the modeled learners using those strategies could infer a lexicon of word forms with associated probabilities of occurrence. We then applied the resulting knowledge to the Rollins corpus subset, letting each strategy segment those utterances as best it could, given the knowledge it had inferred from the training set. The word-object mapping model was then applied with the inferred segmentations as part of the observed input (W). Due to the stochastic nature of the inference process, we repeated this process five times and present averaged results.

We present lexical precision scores due to the importance of inferring high quality mappings during early word meaning learning. However, to measure precision we need to identify what constitutes a "correct" mapping. Frank et al. (2009) created a gold standard referential lexicon by hand and we follow their basic guidelines in creating our own.

One consideration when dealing with non-adult segmentation is the possibility of legitimate mappings between non-words and objects. For instance, the undersegmenation *abunny* might reasonably be mapped onto the object BUNNY. Our gold standard referential lexicon allows these combinations of determiners and content words as legitimate "words" for an object to be mapped to, unlike the original Frank et al. (2009) study. In contrast, an oversgementation like *du* or *ckie* for *duckie* was not allowed as a correct "word" for the object DUCK. This is because neither unit (*du* or *ckie*) captures the true word form. For instance, it isn't good if the child thinks every instance of /ki/ – *key*, *ckie*, etc. – refers to DUCK. Given this, oversegmention errors are worse than undersegmentations, since they damage the ability to form a reasonable word-object mapping.

5.3 Results

Table 4 presents the evaluation results for all modeled learners, including the segmentation word token F-scores, the rate of oversegmentation errors, and the referential lexicon precision scores. We additionally show the word-object mapping results based on the adult orthographic segmentation as an upper-bound comparison.

	Segmentation		Mapping
	F-score	Overseg.	Lex. prec.
Adult Seg	**1.000**	**0.0%**	**0.583**
Batch (Uni)	0.514	1.7%	0.427
Online (Uni)	0.524	9.0%	0.458
Batch (Bi)	0.746	13.8%	0.544
Online (Bi)	0.813	44.8%	0.347
Subtractive Seg	0.833	90.7%	0.336
Random	0.576	53.2%	0.406

Table 4: Average results over five runs from all modeled learners, showing word token F-score segmentation performance, the rate of oversegmentation errors, and the precision of the inferred referential lexicon.

First, we can see that using the adult segmentation yields a referential lexicon with precision 0.583. While this may not seem very high, it is far more precise than other competing word-object mapping strategies investigated by Frank et al. (2009), which had precision scores between 0.06-0.15.

When we turn to the segmentation performance of the learners, we see similar results on the Rollins corpus as we found before. The Bayesian unigram learners have F-scores around 50% (0.514-0.524), which is worse than the random oracle guesser (0.576). In contrast, the Bayesian bigram learners fare much better (0.746-0.813), with almost as good token F-score performance as the subtractive segmenter (0.833).

Interestingly, we see vast differences in the rate of oversegmentation errors. The subtractive segmenter's errors are nearly always oversegmentations (90.7%). The Online Bayesian bigram learner and the random oracle guesser have about half their errors as oversegmentations (44.8%, 53.2%), while the remaining Bayesian learners have very few oversegmentation errors (1.7%-13.8%). Given how damaging oversegmentation errors can be for word-object mapping, we might expect high oversegmentation rates to take their toll despite highly "accurate" word segmentation.

This is precisely what we find for the subtractive segmenter: it has the highest token F-score for segmentation but the worst lexical precision for word-object mappings (0.336). The Online Bayesian bigram learner suffers in lexical precision for a similar reason (0.347), though its oversegmentation bias is lower. Notably, both these learners generate referential lexicons that are worse than what can be achieved by best-case random guessing (0.406). In contrast, the Bayesian learners with very few oversegmentations fare better (0.427-0.544). Given that the best possible performance for lexical precision was 0.583, 0.544 seems quite respectable.

When we examine the mapping errors made by each modeled learner (samples shown in Table 5), the detrimental impact of oversegmentation is more apparent. Notably, many words in English child-directed speech are made up of two syllables (e.g. *birdie*, *bunny*, *piggy*). If these words are oversegmented, the model cannot create a lexical mapping from *birdie* to its object and instead tends to map both *bir* and *die* to the same object. The Bayesian unigram learners never produce these types of oversegmentations for the concrete nouns which the model is attempting to learn (they do, however, produce oversegmentations such as *hip-hop* segmented as *hip* and *hop*). In contrast, the Bayesian bigram learners, the subtractive segmenter, and random oracle learner generate these errors for words that otherwise might have been learned correctly (between 6.4% - 10.2% of all inferred mappings).

	Word	Object	% Over Err
Batch (Bi)	**bu**(nnies)	RABBIT	6.4%
	(bu)**nnies**	RABBIT	
Online (Bi)	(bir)**die**	DUCK	10.2%
	bir(die)	DUCK	
Subtr. Seg	**bu**(nnies)	RABBIT	8.1%
	bir(die)	DUCK	
Random	**pi**(ggy)	PIG	8.5%
	bir(die)	DUCK	

Table 5: Example oversegmentation errors from the four learners that make them for items in the referential lexicon. Oversegmented lexical items are shown in bold with the remainder of the correct word in parentheses. The percentage of all lexical mappings that were incorrect because of oversegmentation is also given.

More generally, similar to the stress utility evaluation, this word-object mapping utility evaluation reveals that segmentations which are more "correct" are not necessarily more useful. In particular, having a non-detrimental segmentation error pattern (i.e., preferring undersegmentation to oversegmentation) may matter more than having a more accurate segmentation for the early stages of both speech segmentation and word-object mapping. However, these results do not necessarily indicate that the online bigram Bayesian or subtractive segmentation strategies are not used by infants. It simply means that if they are, oversegmentations may need to be corrected before word-object mapping can successfully get off the ground. We note that the particular parameters used for the Bayesian strategy can influence the rates of over- and undersegmentation. Because we selected parameters that optimized word token F-score performance, it may be that parameters can be optimized for word-object mapping (and also stress cue induction).

6 Conclusion

We have presented two concrete suggestions for evaluating the utility of speech segmentation strategies, capitalizing on the bootstrapping nature of language acquisition. This utility-focused evaluation approach demonstrates that a more accurate segmentation when compared to a gold standard does not equate to a more useful segmentation for subsequent language acquisition processes. Notably, the types of errors made may significantly impact the utility of the inferred lexicon, so it is worthwhile to analyze not just what is right about a model's output but also exactly what is wrong. This is a specific demonstration of a larger methodological point about how to evaluate unsupervised models of language acquisition. While gold standard evaluation can tell us whether a strategy reproduces adult knowledge, measuring model output utility can indicate what strategies are actually useful for learners.

Acknowledgments

We would like to thank Michael Frank, Ulrike von Luxburg, Sharon Goldwater, Stella Frank, and the members of the Computation of Language Laboratory at UCI for their helpful discussion and comments. This work was supported by a Jean-Claude Falmagne Research Award to the first author from the department of Cognitive Sciences at UCI.

References

Aslin, R., Saffran, J., & Newport, E. (1998). Computation of conditional probability statistics by 8-month-old infants. *Psychological Science*, *9*, 321–324.

Batchelder, E. (2002). Bootstrapping the lexicon: A computational model of infant speech segmentation. *Cognition*, *83*(2), 167–206.

Bergelson, E., & Swingley, D. (2012). At 6–9 months, human infants know the meanings of many common nouns. *Proceedings of the National Academy of Sciences*, *109*(9), 3253–3258.

Bertonicini, J., Bijeljac-Babic, R., Jusczyk, P., Kennedy, L., & Mehler, J. (1988). An investigation of young infants' perceptual representations of speech sounds. *Journal of Experimental Psychology*, *117*(1), 21–33.

Bijeljac-Babic, R., Bertoncini, J., & Mehler, J. (1993). How do 4-day-old infants categorize multisyllabic utterances? *Developmental Psychology*, *29*(4), 711–721.

Blanchard, D., Heinz, J., & Golinkoff, R. (2010). Modeling the contribution of phonotactic cues to the problem of word segmentation. *Journal of child language*, *37*, 487–511.

Börschinger, B., & Johnson, M. (2014). Exploring the role of stress in Bayesian word segmentation using adaptor grammars. *Transactions of the Association for Computational Linguistics*, *2*(1), 93-104.

Bortfeld, H., Morgan, J., Golinkoff, R., & Rathbun, K. (2005). Mommy and me: Familiar names help launch babies into speech-stream segmentation. *Psychological Science*, *16*(4), 298–304.

Brent, M. (1999). An efficient, probabilistically sound algorithm for segmentation and word discovery. *Machine Learning*, *34*, 71–105.

Brown, R. (1973). *A first language: The early stages*. Harvard University Press.

Cole, R., & Jakimik, J. (1980). Perception and production of fluent speech. In R. Cole (Ed.), (pp. 133–163). Hillsdale, NJ: Erlbaum.

Dillon, B., Dunbar, E., & Idsardi, W. (2013). A single-stage approach to learning phonological categories: Insights from inuktitut. *Cognitive Science*, *37*(2), 344–377.

Doyle, G., & Levy, R. (2013). Combining multiple information types in bayesian word segmentation. In *Proceedings of naacl-hlt 2013* (pp. 117–126).

Eimas, P. (1999). Segmental and syllabic representations in the perception of speech by young infants. *Journal of the Acoustical Society of America*, *105*(3), 1901–1911.

Feldman, N., Griffiths, T., Goldwater, S., & Morgan, J. (2013). A role for the developing lexicon in phonetic category acquisition. *Psychological Review*, *120*(4), 751–778.

Ferguson, T. (1973). A bayesian analysis of some nonparametric problems. *Annals of Statistics*, *1*(2), 209–230.

Frank, M., Goodman, N., & Tenenbaum, J. (2009). Using speakers' referential intentions to model early cross-situational word learning. *Psychological Science*, *20*, 579–585.

Geman, S., & Geman, D. (1984). Stochastic relaxation, gibbs distributions, and the bayesian restoration of images. *Pattern Analysis and Machine Intelligence, IEEE Transactions on*, *6*, 721–741.

Goldwater, S., Griffiths, T., & Johnson, M. (2009). A bayesian framework for word segmentation. *Cognition*, *112*(1), 21–54.

Johnson, E., & Jusczyk, P. (2001). Word segmentation by 8-month-olds: When speech cues count more than statistics. *Journal of Memory and Language*, *44*, 548–567.

Jones, B., Johnson, M., & Frank, M. (2010). Learning words and their meanings from unsegmented child-directed speech. In *Human language technologies: The 2010 annual conference of the north american chapter of the association for computational linguistics* (pp. 501–509).

Jusczyk, P., & Derrah, C. (1987). Representation of speech sounds by young infants. *Developmental Psychology*, *23*(5), 648–654.

Jusczyk, P., Hohne, E., & Baumann, A. (1999). Infants' sensitivity to allphonic cues for word segmentation. *Perception and Psychophysics*, *61*, 1465–1476.

Jusczyk, P., Houston, D., & Newsome, M. (1999). The beginnings of word segmentation in

english-learning infants. *Cognitive Psychology, 39*, 159–207.
Kingsbury, P., Strassel, S., McLemore, C., & MacIntyre, R. (1997). *Callhome american english lexicon (pronlex)*. Linguistic Data Consortium.
Landau, B., & Gleitman, L. (1985). *Language and experience*. Cambridge, MA: Harvard University Press.
Lignos, C. (2011). Modeling infant word segmentation. In *Proceedings of the Fifteenth Conference on Computational Natural Language Learning* (pp. 29–38).
Lignos, C. (2012). Infant word segmentation: An incremental, integrated model. In *Proceedings of the 30th west coast conference on formal linguistics* (pp. 237–247).
MacWhinney, B. (2000). *The childes project: Tools for analyzing talk* (3rd ed.). Mahwah, NJ: Lawrence Erlbaum Associates.
Marthi, B., Pasula, H., Russell, S., & Peres, Y. (2002). Decayed mcmc filtering. In *Proceedings of 18th uai* (pp. 319–326).
Mattys, S., Jusczyk, P., & Luce, P. (1999). Phonotactic and prosodic effects on word segmentation in infants. *Cognitive Psychology, 38*, 465–494.
Mercier, C. (1912). *A new logic*. London: William Heineman.
Morgan, J., & Demuth, K. (1996). *Signal to syntax: Bootstrapping from speech to grammar in early acquisition*. Lawrence Erlbaum Associates, Inc.
Morgan, J., & Saffran, J. (1995). Emerging integration of sequential and suprasegmental information in preverbal speech segmentation. *Child Development, 66*(4), 911–936.
Pearl, L., Goldwater, S., & Steyvers, M. (2011). Online learning mechanisms for bayesian models of word segmentation. *Research on Language and Computation, 8*(2), 107–132. (special issue on computational models of language acquisition)
Pelucchi, B., Hay, J., & Saffran, J. (2009). Learning in reverse: Eight-month-old infants track backward transitional probabilities. *Cognition, 113*, 244–247.
Perfors, A., Ransom, K., & Navarro, D. (2014). People ignore token frequency when deciding how widely to generalize. In *Proceedings of the 36th Annual Conference of the Cognitive Science Society* (pp. 2759–2764).
Peters, A. (1983). *The units of language acquisition*. New York: Cambridge University Press.
Phillips, L., & Pearl, L. (2014a). Bayesian inference as a cross-linguistic word segmentation strategy: Always learning useful things. In *Proceedings of the Computational and Cognitive Models of Language Acquisition and Language Processing Workshop*.
Phillips, L., & Pearl, L. (2014b). Bayesian inference as a viable cross-linguistic word segmentation strategy: It's about what's useful. In *Proceedings of the 36th annual conference of the cognitive science society*.
Phillips, L., & Pearl, L. (in press). The utility of cognitive plausibility in language acquisition modeling: Evidence from word segmentation. *Cognitive Science*.
Saffran, J., Aslin, R., & Newport, E. (1996). Statistical learning by 8-month-old infants. *Science, 274*, 1926–1928.
Teh, Y., Jordan, M., Beal, M., & Blei, D. (2006). Heirarchical dirichlet processes. *Journal of the American Statistical Association, 101*(476), 1566–1581.
Theodoridis, S., & Koutroubas, K. (1999). *Pattern recognition*. Academic Press.
Thiessen, E., & Saffran, J. (2003). When cues collide: Use of stress and statistical cues to word boundaries by 7- to 9-month-old infants. *Developmental Psychology, 39*(4), 706–716.
Tincoff, R., & Jusczyk, P. W. (1999). Some beginnings of word comprehension in 6-month-olds. *Psychological Science, 10*(2), 172–175.
Tincoff, R., & Jusczyk, P. W. (2012). Six-month-olds comprehend words that refer to parts of the body. *Infancy, 17*(4), 432–444.
von Luxburg, U., Williamson, R., & Guyon, I. (2011). Clustering: Science or art? In *JMLR Workshop and Conference Proceedings 27* (pp. 65–79). (Workshop on Unsupervised Learning and Transfer Learning)
Yang, C. (2005). On productivity. *Linguistic variation yearbook, 5*(1), 265–302.

Evidence of syntactic working memory usage in MEG data

Marten van Schijndel
Department of Linguistics
The Ohio State University
vanschm@ling.osu.edu

Brian Murphy*
School of Electronics,
Electrical Engineering and Computer Science
Queen's University Belfast
brian.murphy@qub.ac.uk

William Schuler
Department of Linguistics
The Ohio State University
schuler.77@osu.edu

Abstract

While reading times are often used to measure working memory load, frequency effects (such as surprisal or *n*-gram frequencies) also have strong confounding effects on reading times. This work uses a naturalistic audio corpus with magnetoencephalographic (MEG) annotations to measure working memory load during sentence processing. Alpha oscillations in posterior regions of the brain have been found to correlate with working memory load in non-linguistic tasks (Jensen et al., 2002), and the present study extends these findings to working memory load caused by syntactic center embeddings. Moreover, this work finds that frequency effects in naturally-occurring stimuli do not significantly contribute to neural oscillations in any frequency band, which suggests that many modeling claims could be tested on this sort of data even without controlling for frequency effects.

1 Introduction

Current accounts of sentence processing (e.g., Gibson, 2000; Lewis and Vasishth, 2005) usually involve working memory: parts of sentences are stored while unrelated material is processed, then retrieved when they can be integrated. But evidence for the role of memory in sentence processing usually comes in the form of latency measurements in self-paced reading or eye-tracking data, in which frequency effects are a powerful potential confound (Hale, 2001; Levy, 2008; Demberg and Keller, 2008; Roark et al., 2009; Smith and Levy, 2013; van Schijndel et al., 2014). For example, the direction of the correlation between memory load and reading times has been shown to be highly sensitive to complex frequency effects (Vasishth and Lewis, 2006; Schuler and van Schijndel, 2014).

Experiments described in this paper therefore attempt to find a clearer measure of variable memory usage in sentence processing, independent of frequency influences. In particular, this paper focuses on the coherence of oscillatory neural activity between anterior and posterior areas of left cortex. Areas including the left inferior frontal gyrus and the posterior left temporal cortex have been implicated in language use, especially passive listening tasks (Hagoort and Indefrey, 2014). Synchronous firing among neurons in disparate parts of the brain is thought to be a possible mechanism for the formation of cued associations in memory by causing rapidly repeated communication between association cue neurons and association target neurons, which strengthens their connection through a process of long-term potentiation (von der Malsburg, 1995; Singer, 1999; Sederberg et al., 2003; Jensen et al., 2007; Fell and Axmacher, 2011). During periods of high memory load, synchronous firing in the alpha band is thought to be associated with inhibition of memory formation so as to protect existing cues from interference (Jensen et al., 2002; Jensen et al., 2007). If this is correct, we should expect to find high alpha power and coherence among brain regions responsible for language use when language users are processing center embedded text (e.g., the bracketed text in 'The reporter [the senator

* Formerly of the Dept. of Machine Learning, Carnegie Mellon University

Proceedings of CMCL 2015, pages 79–88,
Denver, Colorado, June 4, 2015.

met] left'). Magnetoencephalographic (MEG) imaging results reported in this paper show that this does indeed seem to be the case. Exploratory analyses with the development partition of a dataset of MEG recordings of subjects listening to narrative text revealed a strong effect for memory load on alpha-band coherence between an anterior and posterior pair of left-hemisphere sensors. Follow-on validation with a larger test partition confirmed the significance of this effect. Moreover, these effects could not be explained by frequency or sentence position predictors, unlike effects on self-paced reading and eye-tracking latencies (Demberg and Keller, 2008; Roark et al., 2009; Wu et al., 2010).

The remainder of this paper is organized as follows: Section 2 provides a brief introduction to magnetoencephalography, Section 3 describes the MEG dataset used in these experiments, Section 4 describes the oscillatory coherence measure used to evaluate phase-aligned activation, Section 5 describes the center-embedding depth predictor, Section 6 describes the regression experiments and their results, and Section 7 discusses implications of these results for some open debates about hierarchic sentence processing.

2 MEG Background

Magnetoencephalography (MEG), like electroencephalography (EEG), is a non-invasive means to record the electrical activity of the brain, specifically the aggregate of post-synaptic potentials produced by individual neurons. MEG has certain advantages over EEG, which is the most widely used neuroimaging technique in psycholinguistics, due to its low cost, convenience and portability. While EEG's high temporal resolution ($\gg$100Hz) makes it suitable for examining the neural processing timeline down to the level of individual words and phonemes, its spatial resolution does not compare to other techniques like fMRI (functional magnetic resonance imaging). In addition, the signals recorded with EEG (volume currents) are distorted as they pass through the skull and tissues of the head, attenuating higher frequencies, and blurring their spatial source.

MEG records magnetic fields from the same neural sources that generate the EEG-visible voltages at the scalp. As the head is transparent to magnetic fields, MEG signals are less noisy, have finer spatial resolution, and capture a wider range of frequencies. The EEG signal components familiar to psycholinguists (e.g., the N400 and P600) are also visible but produce different scalp distributions in MEG recordings (Pylkkänen and Marantz, 2003; Salmelin, 2007; Service et al., 2007), because of differing spatial sensitivities: EEG and MEG are more sensitive to radial and tangential sources respectively, and MEG's higher spatial resolution means that it is not as sensitive to deep sources. And correspondingly, any magnetic coherence between two sensors can be more reliably traced to coherence between the two corresponding regions of the brain, whereas the poor spatial resolution of EEG means that coherence between sensors does not necessarily reflect coherence between the corresponding regions of the brain.

3 Data Collection

This study makes use of a naturalistic audio-book listening task during MEG recording. This design allows us to examine language processing in a more ecologically realistic manner (Brennan et al., 2012; Wehbe et al., 2014a; Wehbe et al., 2014b), as both the participant experience (reading/listening to a story for enjoyment) and author's aim are authentic language acts.

Participants were asked to sit still in an upright position with their eyes closed, while they listened to an 80-minute excerpt of an English-language novel. The listening task was split into 8 sections of approximately 10 minutes each, and participants had the opportunity to rest between them.

The text used was the second chapter of the novel *Heart of Darkness* by Joseph Conrad, containing 628 sentences and 12,342 word tokens. The plain-text and audio book recording used were both sourced from the Gutenberg project.[1]

The data was recorded at 1000Hz on a 306-channel Elekta Neuromag device at the UPMC MEG Brain Mapping Center, Pittsburgh, USA. During the experiment, the audio track was recorded in parallel to enable subsequent synchronization between the brain activity and audio-book content.

[1]http://www.gutenberg.org/cache/epub/219/pg219.txt; http://www.gutenberg.org/ebooks/20270

The 306 channels are distributed across 102 locations in the device helmet. Each position has a magnetometer which measures the magnitude of the magnetic flux entering or leaving the helmet at that location. The two gradiometers measure gradients in local flux (i.e. its first derivative), each in a direction perpendicular to the other.

Informed consent was obtained from 3 healthy right-handed participants, following ethical approval provided by the Institutional Review Boards of both the University of Pittsburgh, and Carnegie Mellon University.

After recording, the MEG data was preprocessed in the following way to normalize and clean the signals. The Elekta custom MaxFilter software was used to apply SSP, SSS and tSSS methods (Taulu and Hari, 2009), correcting for head motion on a run-wise basis, and removing signal components which originated outside the recording helmet and other non-brain artefacts. The EEGlab package was then used to apply a band-pass filter between 0.01–50 Hz, down-sample to 125Hz, and apply Independent Components Analysis (Delorme and Makeig, 2003). The signal time-courses and component scalp-maps were visually inspected for eye-movement and line-noise components, but none were identified.

The parallel audio recording channel was used to identify the precise sample points at which each of the 8 audio runs began and ended (these varied as participants chose to take breaks of different lengths). The eight excerpts were then spliced together to form a continuous set of MEG signals corresponding exactly to the complete audio-book time-course. This allowed us to use speech recognition forced alignment methods (MS HTK; Woodland et al., 1994) to precisely locate the onset and offset times of each auditory word. These automatically derived onset and offset times were subsequently validated by hand.

4 Coherence

There are a variety of measures available that reflect the connectivity between two brain regions. This study makes use of 'spectral coherence,' which is sensitive both to power/energy increases registered by the relevant sensors and to the degree of phase synchronization observed by those sensors. Spectral coherence is computed with the following formula:

$$\text{coherence}(x, y) = \frac{\mathrm{E}[S_{xy}]}{\sqrt{\mathrm{E}[S_{xx}] \cdot \mathrm{E}[S_{yy}]}} \quad (1)$$

where x and y are waveform signals from two sensors, and S_{ij} is the spectral density of waveforms i and j. When $i = j$, S is the power spectral density of i, and when $i \neq j$, S is the cross-spectral density between i and j. The expectations in the numerator and the denominator must be obtained by averaging over multiple frequency bands, multiple instances of the same frequency band in different epochs, or over both frequency bands and epochs.[2] The present work adopts the second approach of averaging each frequency band over multiple epochs (see Section 6 for details), which enables higher frequency resolution than if multiple frequencies had been averaged together, though it necessarily reduces the number of trials in the dataset. This work uses the MNE-python package to compute spectral coherence (Gramfort et al., 2013; Gramfort et al., 2014).[3]

As a measure of the correlation between two signals, coherence can be between 0 and 1. When two signals have a constant phase difference and are of the same amplitude, their coherence is 1. As either the amplitudes diverge or the phase difference changes, the coherence approaches 0.

5 Center Embedding Depth

This study evaluates a measure of syntactic working memory load as a predictor of MEG coherence. A canonical means of calculating syntactic working memory load is to count the number of center embeddings in a sentence. For example, the sentence in Figure 1, 'The cart that the horse that the man bought pulled broke,' is thought to induce greater working memory load than the same sentence without the depth 3 region: 'The cart that the horse pulled broke,' (Chomsky and Miller, 1963).[4] The increased memory load stems from an incomplete dependency (a subject lacking a predicate in the above

[2] If multiple instances are not averaged in Equation 1, coherence is simply 1 (Benignus, 1969).

[3] http://martinos.org/mne/stable/mne-python.html

[4] In fact, this is an example of *self embedding*, the most difficult form of center embedding, which was chosen for ease of exposition.

$d1$ The cart				broke.
$d2$	that the horse		pulled	
$d3$		that the man bought		

Figure 1: Center embeddings in 'The cart that the horse that the man bought pulled broke.' Each lexeme is associated with the given embedding depth on the left.

example) that must be retained in working memory until the dependency can be completed (Gibson, 2000). The load should increase every time there is a right branch from a left branch in a syntactic binary-branching tree.[5]

Experiments described in this paper estimate syntactic memory load when processing a particular word of a sentence as the center-embedding depth of that word, which is the number of incomplete categories maintained while processing that word using a left-corner parser (Aho and Ullman, 1972; Johnson-Laird, 1983; Abney and Johnson, 1991; Gibson, 1991; Resnik, 1992; Stabler, 1994). To obtain an accurate estimate of center-embedding depth, this study uses the van Schijndel et al. (2013) left-corner PCFG parser trained on the Penn Treebank (Marcus et al., 1993) reannotated into a Nguyen et al. (2012) generalized categorial grammar (GCG),[6] which makes PCFG probabilities sensitive to filler-gap propagation. This parser achieves a linguistic accuracy comparable to the Petrov and Klein (2007) parser, and the PCFG surprisal estimates it outputs using this grammar provide a state-of-the-art fit to psycholinguistic measures like self-paced reading times and eye-tracking fixation durations (van Schijndel and Schuler, 2015).

The experiments described in Section 6 run this parser on transcripts of the *Heart of Darkness* dataset described in Section 3, calculating center-embedding depth for each word epoch based on its position in the best output parse. This parser is also used to calculate PCFG surprisal as a potentially confounding predictor.

[5] In fact, there are conditions where a post-modifier can create a complex left-branching structure that does not cause an associated increase in memory load, but that effect is beyond the scope of this paper.

[6] http://sourceforge.net/projects/modelblocks/

6 Methodology

In this section we describe how we establish a reliable effect of sentence embedding depth on alpha-band coherence in the MEG recordings. While our analysis is motivated by experimental results using non-linguistic stimuli (e.g., Jensen et al., 2002), we do not expect the scalp topology of EEG effects to be exactly replicated in MEG recordings, and we do not necessarily expect coherence observations during skilled behavior like sentence comprehension to exactly match observations while processing word lists. This, and the possibility of frequency-based confounds, requires an exploratory analysis of a range of sensor-pairs, frequency bands, and time windows. To avoid the danger of selection biases we partition one third of the data into a development set and the rest of the data into a test set. The development data gives an indication of which sensor pair best reflects a stable correlation between embedding depth and MEG coherence, which is later confirmed using the test partition.

The van Schijndel et al. (2013) parser is used to obtain estimates of the embedding depth of each word in the corpus according to the best output parse of the sentence. As described in Section 5, these estimates are used as a measure of the memory load that is present as each word is processed.

The data is divided into epochs, which extend from one second pre-onset to two seconds post-onset for each word. This window extends beyond the average auditory duration of a word ($\sim$0.4s), and assumes that the processing timeline for each word is time-locked to its auditory onset (Hagoort, 2008). In order to clean up extraneous noise in the signal, words are omitted if they are in a sentence that fails to parse, if they are in an extremely short or an extremely long sentence ($<$4 or $>$50 words), or if they follow a word at a different depth, which could introduce a possible confound due to storage or integration effects (Gibson, 2000). The remaining sentences should provide regions where the parser is confident about its depth estimates, where sentence length is unexceptional, and where linguistic memory load is not changing. Every third sentence is put into the exploratory development dataset, and the rest are put into the test set. For each dataset, the epochs are grouped based on their associated em-

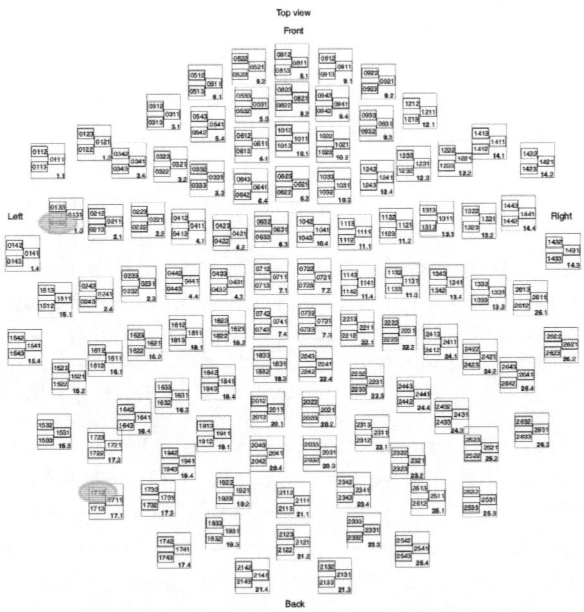

Figure 2: Top-down depiction of sensor locations in the Elekta Neuromag helmet. The front of the helmet is at the top of the figure. The sensors in blue are those used in this study.

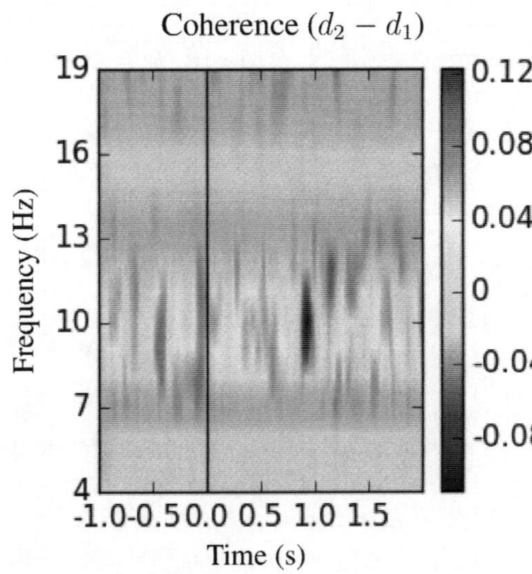

Figure 3: A time-frequency depiction of the mean coherence in the depth = 1 condition subtracted from the mean coherence in the depth = 2 condition in development data. An overlay conveys the variance of different frequency bands. Faded regions have higher variance than clearer regions.

bedding depths. Each depth grouping is further clustered into sets of four epochs; these sets are used to calculate the expectations necessary to compute coherence.[7] Continuous wavelet decomposition (Gabor, 1946) is employed to decompose the waveform signal recorded by each sensor into its component frequencies.

The memory load of a given epoch should be relatively constant throughout the duration of a given word, so the dependent variable tested in this study is the average coherence from 0-500 ms after the onset of each word. If the average coherence of a frequency is high due to a brief spike in coherence during that window rather than due to repeated synchronous firing of the neural clusters under investigation, the increased variance will penalize the significance of that frequency. Although this work initially averaged over epochs during computation of coherence in order to obtain good frequency resolution, exploration using development data revealed that coherence often appears across several adjacent frequency bands, so to boost the signal-to-noise ratio, the dependent variable was recast as the average coherence within ± 2 Hz of each frequency band. Since this study is focused on linguistic processing, the development data was searched for two sensors in the anterior and posterior regions of the left hemisphere with a high degree of depth-sensitive alpha coherence. In analysis of the development set, gradiometer sensors 0132 and 1712 (anterior and posterior sensors, respectively; shown in Figure 2) showed a high coherence, so these were used in the evaluation on the test set. This was the only sensor pair evaluated on the test data.

To avoid making the statistical analyses vulnerable to assumptions about data distribution, statistical significance of depth as a predictor in the development and test datasets is calculated using the Mann-Whitney U-test, a non-parametric alternative to the t-test for testing differences between two unpaired

[7] The choice to cluster into sets of four epochs was driven by the data. In order to obtain valid statistical significance in the development data regarding embeddings at an embedding depth of one, the data could only be divided by 4 before n dropped below 30. While statistical significance is not needed for exploration, a less-than-representative sample in the development set would negate the purpose of having a development set for exploration.

Factor	Coef	p-value
Unigram	$5.1 \cdot 10^{-5}$	0.941
Bigram	$5.6 \cdot 10^{-4}$	0.257
Trigram	$4.3 \cdot 10^{-4}$	0.073
PCFG Surprisal	$2.8 \cdot 10^{-4}$	0.482
Sentence Position	$-5.1 \cdot 10^{-4}$	0.031
Depth	$3.6 \cdot 10^{-2}$	0.005

Table 1: Development data results using each factor to predict alpha coherence from 0-500ms at 10±2Hz.

Factor	Coef	p-value
Unigram	$-2.2 \cdot 10^{-4}$	0.6480
Bigram	$-9.8 \cdot 10^{-5}$	0.7762
Trigram	$3.7 \cdot 10^{-4}$	0.0264
PCFG Surprisal	$2.9 \cdot 10^{-4}$	0.3295
Sentence Position	$1.3 \cdot 10^{-4}$	0.4628
Depth	$4.6 \cdot 10^{-2}$	0.00002

Table 2: Test data results using each factor to predict alpha coherence from 0-500ms at 10±2Hz. Note that the trigram factor is not a significant predictor after applying Bonferroni correction.

samples. The U-test is used to see whether the distribution of coherence at a given depth is the same as the distribution of coherence at another depth.

Development analysis finds that the depth 1 data ($n = 40$) and the depth 2 data ($n = 1118$) have significantly different coherence distributions around 10 Hz ($p = 0.005$; see Figure 3), which is in the middle of the alpha frequency range (8-12Hz). This finding suggests that alpha coherence between these two regions are predictive of linguistic working memory load. To ensure that this finding was not caused by a single subject, the same analysis was repeated over the development data after omitting each subject in turn, with similar results.

It may be, however, that these alpha coherence effects are driven by confounding factors like sentence position (alpha coherence may be more likely to occur near the beginnings or ends of sentences) or frequency (alpha coherence may tend to increase when processing rare or common words), which may be collinear with depth. In order to check for these possible confounds, the data must be re-ordered by sentence position or frequency predictors, then regrouped into sets of four before computing coherence, in order to avoid computing coherence over unrelated factor levels.[8]

To rule out the confounds of sentence position and frequency, a variety of independent predictors are separately linearly regressed against the dependent variable of coherence. Four different frequency predictors are used: unigrams, bigrams, trigrams, and PCFG surprisal. The n-gram factors are all log-probabilities computed from the Corpus of Contemporary American English (COCA; Davies, 2008) and PCFG surprisal is computed by the van Schijndel et al. (2013) incremental parser. While sentence position is significant on the development partition (Table 1), none of the frequency-based effects are significant in the development set, but this may be due to having too little data in the development set, so all factors are tested again in the larger test set.[9]

To retain an α-level of 0.05 with six statistical tests, the threshold for significance must be Bonferroni corrected to 0.008. As shown in Table 2, sentence position fails to be a significant predictor of alpha coherence on the test data (even without Bonferroni correction), but embedding depth remains a significant predictor of alpha coherence. The marginal effect of trigram predictability observed in the development set remains in the test set, but the effect is not significant after correcting for multiple comparisons.

While Bonferroni correction would rule out trigram probability as a significant predictor even if it was the only non-depth predictor tested in this work, the fact that it is marginally significant in both datasets is suggestive of a true underlying effect. To determine whether trigram probability is actually predictive of MEG coherence, we increase the resolution of the coherence by using six epochs (rather than the previous four) to compute the expectations in Equation 1. The increase in resolution further

[8]Since only two values of depth are tested in the present study, depth is always tested using a U-test, while the more continuous variables are tested using linear regression.

[9]In development testing, 'significance' is merely a convenient tool for summarizing how strongly correlated the independent and dependent variables are. The general lack of correlation between MEG coherence and position/frequency predictors in development data suggests this is a promising dependent variable for our purposes.

Factor	Coef	p-value
Trigram	$1.6 \cdot 10^{-4}$	0.3817
Depth	$3.2 \cdot 10^{-2}$	0.0046

Table 3: Test data results after increasing coherence resolution to six epochs.

shrinks the dataset, but the larger test set can absorb the loss and still provide valid significance results.[10] The results (Table 3) show that, with greater coherence resolution, embedding depth remains a significant predictor of MEG coherence, and that trigram probability is not even a marginally significant predictor. These results reinforce the theory that alpha coherence reflects memory load and further shows that alpha coherence between the anterior and posterior regions of the left hemisphere may specifically reflect linguistic memory load.

7 Discussion

This study found that alpha coherence between the anterior and posterior regions of the left hemisphere of the brain is significantly correlated with embedding depth, which suggests that alpha coherence may reflect an effect of memory load on linguistic processing in those regions. This correlation was found in an exploratory study using development data and subsequently confirmed by generalizing to held-out test data. These results are consistent with patterns observed in fMRI experiments: a large survey (Hagoort and Indefrey, 2014) identifies activation of the left inferior frontal gyrus (LIFG, including "Broca's area") and posterior parts of the left temporal cortex (including "Wernicke's area"), during both passive listening and passive reading tasks. Their findings indicate that, with listening tasks in particular, the anterior region of the right hemisphere is also active, and the results of Weiss et al. (2005) suggest that EEG coherence between the left and right hemispheres of the brain increases with embedding depth. Future study is needed to determine if rightside coherence or left-right coherence in MEG data is also associated with embedding depth.

Importantly, the alpha coherence found in this study did not correlate with sentence position or frequency effects. The lack of influence of position and frequency effects on MEG coherence could greatly facilitate future research on sentence processing, since these effects often present large confounds in predicting other psycholinguistic measures. The cost associated with collecting MEG data may limit the immediate widespread application of the present findings, but since MEG and EEG signals are produced by electrical activity from the same underlying brain sources, this gives hope that anterior-posterior left hemisphere alpha coherence in EEG may be able to provide a similarly clear signal for future studies.

The present data support findings like those of van Schijndel and Schuler (2015), who claim hierarchic structure must be used during linguistic processing because hierarchic structure improves the fit to reading times over competitive non-hierarchic models. A potential criticism of that finding is that humans may make use of linear sequences of part-of-speech tags but not hierarchic structure during linguistic processing (Frank and Bod, 2011). In that case, the improved fit of the hierarchic grammars in van Schijndel and Schuler (2015) may simply stem from the fact that hierarchic grammars also happen to contain part-of-speech information as well as hierarchic structure. The findings of the present study support the theory that hierarchic structure is used during linguistic processing since this study finds a clear effect of alpha coherence conditioned on hierarchic embedding depth.

Having identified a working-memory based signal that is seemingly free of many of the confounding influences associated with reading times, it should be interesting to use the same procedure to study linguistic regions where embedding depth changes. Such studies could tell us what activation patterns arise due to storage and integration of linguistic elements in working memory. Contrary to the previous studies of such influences, which relied on indirect measures such as reading time latencies, if coherence is construed as attentional focus (Jensen et al., 2007), the present methods could directly investigate theoretical claims such as those made by Gibson (2000) and Lewis et al. (2006) regarding the attentional resources required for storage and integration of incomplete dependencies under different

[10] After increasing coherence resolution, trigram $n = 1933$, depth 1 $n = 57$, and depth 2 $n = 1428$.

conditions. That is, it permits direct measurement of whether and how much attentional resources must be expended in cohering disparate regions of the brain in those conditions. Such resource expenditures could manifest themselves in reading times in a variety of ways, but the present work has outlined a technique, seemingly independent of frequency effects, of directly testing the underlying theoretical linguistic claims in naturalistic data.

Acknowledgements

Thanks to the anonymous reviewers for their helpful feedback on this work. Thanks also to Roberto Zamparelli of the University of Trento, for advice on the pilot experimental and analytical design. This material is based upon work supported by the National Science Foundation Graduate Research Fellowship under Grant No. DGE-1343012. Support also came from the University of Pittsburgh Medical Center MEG Seed Fund, and the National Institutes of Health CRCNS grant No. 5R01HD075328-02. Any opinion, findings, and conclusions or recommendations expressed in this material are those of the authors and do not necessarily reflect the views of the funders.

References

Steven P. Abney and Mark Johnson. 1991. Memory requirements and local ambiguities of parsing strategies. *J. Psycholinguistic Research*, 20(3):233–250.

Alfred V. Aho and Jeffery D. Ullman. 1972. *The Theory of Parsing, Translation and Compiling; Volume. I: Parsing*. Prentice-Hall, Englewood Cliffs, New Jersey.

V. A. Benignus. 1969. Estimation of the coherence spectrum and its confidence interval using the fast Fourier transform. *IEEE Transactions on Audio and Electroacoustics*, 17(2):145–150.

Jonathan Brennan, Yuval Nir, Uri Hasson, Rafael Malach, David J Heeger, and Liina Pylkkänen. 2012. Syntactic structure building in the anterior temporal lobe during natural story listening. *Brain and Language*, 120(2):163–173.

Noam Chomsky and George A. Miller. 1963. Introduction to the formal analysis of natural languages. In *Handbook of Mathematical Psychology*, pages 269–321. Wiley, New York, NY.

Mark Davies. 2008. The corpus of contemporary american english: 450 million words, 1990-present.

Arnaud Delorme and Scott Makeig. 2003. EEGLAB: an open source toolbox for analysis of single-trial dynamics including independent component analysis. *Journal of Neuroscience Methods*, 134(1):9–21, mar.

Vera Demberg and Frank Keller. 2008. Data from eye-tracking corpora as evidence for theories of syntactic processing complexity. *Cognition*, 109(2):193–210.

Juergen Fell and Nikolai Axmacher. 2011. The role of phase synchronization in memory processes. *Nature Reviews Neuroscience*, 12(2):105–118.

Stefan Frank and Rens Bod. 2011. Insensitivity of the human sentence-processing system to hierarchical structure. *Psychological Science*.

Dennis Gabor. 1946. Theory of communication. *Journal of the IEEE*, 93:429–441.

Edward Gibson. 1991. *A computational theory of human linguistic processing: Memory limitations and processing breakdown*. Ph.D. thesis, Carnegie Mellon.

Edward Gibson. 2000. The dependency locality theory: A distance-based theory of linguistic complexity. In *Image, language, brain: Papers from the first mind articulation project symposium*, pages 95–126, Cambridge, MA. MIT Press.

A. Gramfort, M. Luessi, E. Larson, D. Engemann, D. Strohmeier, C. Brodbeck, R. Goj, M. Jas, T. Brooks, L. Parkkonen, and M. Hämäläinen. 2013. MEG and EEG data analysis with MNE-python. *Frontiers in Neuroscience*, 7:267.

A. Gramfort, M. Luessi, E. Larson, D. Engemann, D. Strohmeier, C. Brodbeck, L. Parkkonen, and M. Hämäläinen. 2014. MNE software for processing MEG and EEG data. *NeuroImage*, 86:446–460.

Peter Hagoort and Peter Indefrey. 2014. The neurobiology of language beyond single words. *Annual Review of Neuroscience*, 37:347–362.

Peter Hagoort. 2008. The fractionation of spoken language understanding by measuring electrical and magnetic brain signals. *Philosophical Transactions of the Royal Society B: Biological Sciences*, 363(1493):1055–1069, mar.

John Hale. 2001. A probabilistic earley parser as a psycholinguistic model. In *Proceedings of the second meeting of the North American chapter of the Association for Computational Linguistics*, pages 159–166, Pittsburgh, PA.

Ole Jensen, Jack Gelfand, John Kounios, and John E. Lisman. 2002. Oscillations in the alpha band (9–12 hz) increase with memory load during retention in a short-term memory task. *Cerebral Cortex*.

Ole Jensen, Jochen Kaiser, and Jean-Philippe Lachaux. 2007. Human gamma-frequency oscillations associated with attention and memory. *Trends in Neurosciences*, 30(7):317–324.

Philip N. Johnson-Laird. 1983. *Mental models: towards a cognitive science of language, inference, and consciousness*. Harvard University Press, Cambridge, MA, USA.

Roger Levy. 2008. Expectation-based syntactic comprehension. *Cognition*, 106(3):1126–1177.

Richard L. Lewis and Shravan Vasishth. 2005. An activation-based model of sentence processing as skilled memory retrieval. *Cognitive Science*, 29(3):375–419.

Richard L. Lewis, Shravan Vasishth, and Julie A. Van Dyke. 2006. Computational principles of working memory in sentence comprehension. *Trends in Cognitive Science*, 10(10):447–454.

Mitchell P. Marcus, Beatrice Santorini, and Mary Ann Marcinkiewicz. 1993. Building a large annotated corpus of English: the Penn Treebank. *Computational Linguistics*, 19(2):313–330.

Luan Nguyen, Marten van Schijndel, and William Schuler. 2012. Accurate unbounded dependency recovery using generalized categorial grammars. In *Proceedings of the 24th International Conference on Computational Linguistics (COLING '12)*, pages 2125–2140, Mumbai, India.

Slav Petrov and Dan Klein. 2007. Improved inference for unlexicalized parsing. In *Proceedings of NAACL HLT 2007*, pages 404–411, Rochester, New York, April. Association for Computational Linguistics.

Liina Pylkkänen and Alec Marantz. 2003. Tracking the time course of word recognition with MEG. *Trends in cognitive sciences*, 7(5):187–189.

Philip Resnik. 1992. Left-corner parsing and psychological plausibility. In *Proceedings of COLING*, pages 191–197, Nantes, France.

Brian Roark, Asaf Bachrach, Carlos Cardenas, and Christophe Pallier. 2009. Deriving lexical and syntactic expectation-based measures for psycholinguistic modeling via incremental top-down parsing. *Proceedings of the 2009 Conference on Empirical Methods in Natural Langauge Processing*, pages 324–333.

Riitta Salmelin. 2007. Clinical neurophysiology of language: the MEG approach. *Clinical neurophysiology : official journal of the International Federation of Clinical Neurophysiology*, 118(2):237–54, mar.

William Schuler and Marten van Schijndel. 2014. Effects of integration in eye tracking. In *Twenty-Seventh Annual CUNY Conference on Human Sentence Processing*, page 207.

Per B Sederberg, Michael J Kahana, Marc W Howard, Elizabeth J Donner, and Joseph R Madsen. 2003. Theta and gamma oscillations during encoding predict subsequent recall. *The Journal of Neuroscience*, 23(34):10809–10814.

Elisabet Service, Päivi Helenius, Sini Maury, and Riitta Salmelin. 2007. Localization of Syntactic and Semantic Brain Responses using Magnetoencephalography. *Journal of Cognitive Neuroscience*, 19(7):1193–1205.

Wolf Singer. 1999. Neuronal synchrony: A versatile code for the definition of relations? *Neuron*, 24(1):49–65.

Nathaniel J. Smith and Roger Levy. 2013. The effect of word predictability on reading time is logarithmic. *Cognition*, 128:302–319.

Edward Stabler. 1994. The finite connectivity of linguistic structure. In *Perspectives on Sentence Processing*, pages 303–336. Lawrence Erlbaum.

Samu Taulu and Riitta Hari. 2009. Removal of magnetoencephalographic artifacts with temporal signal-space separation: demonstration with single-trial auditory-evoked responses. *Human Brain Mapping*, 30:1524–1534.

Marten van Schijndel and William Schuler. 2015. Hierarchic syntax improves reading time prediction. In *Proceedings of NAACL-HLT 2015*. Association for Computational Linguistics.

Marten van Schijndel, Andy Exley, and William Schuler. 2013. A model of language processing as hierarchic sequential prediction. *Topics in Cognitive Science*, 5(3):522–540.

Marten van Schijndel, William Schuler, and Peter W Culicover. 2014. Frequency effects in the processing of unbounded dependencies. In *Proc. of CogSci 2014*. Cognitive Science Society.

Shravan Vasishth and Richard L. Lewis. 2006. Argument-head distance and processing complexity: Explaining both locality and antilocality effects. *Language*, 82(4):767–794.

Christoph von der Malsburg. 1995. Binding in models of perception and brain function. In *Current Opinion in Neurobiology*, pages 520–526.

Leila Wehbe, Brian Murphy, Partha Talukdar, Alona Fyshe, Aaditya Ramdas, and Tom Mitchell. 2014a. Simultaneously uncovering the patterns of brain regions involved in different story reading subprocesses. *PloS one*, 9(11):e112575.

Leila Wehbe, Ashish Vaswani, Kevin Knight, and Tom Mitchell. 2014b. Aligning context-based statistical models of language with brain activity during reading. In *Proceedings of the 2014 Conference on Empirical Methods in Natural Language Processing*. ACL.

Sabine Weiss, Horst M. Mueller, Baerbel Schack, Jonathan W. King, Martha Kutas, and Peter Rappelsberger. 2005. Increased neuronal communication accompanying sentence comprehension. *International Journal of Psychophysiology*, 57:129–141.

P.C. Woodland, J.J. Odell, V. Valtchev, and S.J. Young. 1994. Large vocabulary continuous speech recognition using HTK. In *Proceedings of ICASSP '94. IEEE International Conference on Acoustics, Speech and Signal Processing*, volume ii, pages II/125–II/128. IEEE.

Stephen Wu, Asaf Bachrach, Carlos Cardenas, and William Schuler. 2010. Complexity metrics in an incremental right-corner parser. In *Proceedings of the 48th Annual Meeting of the Association for Computational Linguistics (ACL'10)*, pages 1189–1198.

Modeling fMRI time courses with linguistic structure at various grain sizes

John T. Hale and **David E. Lutz** and **Wen-Ming Luh**
Cornell University
Ithaca, NY 14853 USA
{jthale,del82,wenmingluh}@cornell.edu

Jonathan R. Brennan
The University of Michigan
Ann Arbor, MI 48109 USA
jobrenn@umich.edu

Abstract

Neuroimaging while participants listen to audiobooks provides a rich data source for theories of incremental parsing. We compare nested regression models of these data. These mixed-effects models incorporate linguistic predictors at various grain sizes ranging from part-of-speech bigrams, through surprisal on context-free treebank grammars, to incremental node counts in trees that are derived by Minimalist Grammars. The fine-grained structures make an independent contribution over and above coarser predictors. However, this result only obtains with time courses from anterior temporal lobe (aTL). In analogous time courses from inferior frontal gyrus, only n-grams improve upon a non-syntactic baseline. These results support the idea that aTL does combinatoric processing during naturalistic story comprehension, processing that bears a systematic relationship to linguistic structure.

1 Introduction

The cognitive science of language confronts two different notions of its own subject matter. One notion is rooted in the psychology of an individual: what states of mind does *this* person go through as he or she uses language? The other notion starts from languages themselves. As a structural system, how does *this* language differ from another? There is a tension between these two views. Classically, this tension is resolved by adopting the Competence Hypothesis (Chomsky, 1965, page 9). It suggests that the best description of the language system should also figure as a "basic component" in the best description of the language-user. This Hypothesis is programmatic enough to have received several different interpretations over the years (Bresnan and Kaplan, 1982; Steedman, 1989; Stabler, 1991). Can a refined version of it be accepted or rejected in light of experimental data?

Recent work with eye-tracking has wrestled with just this question (Frank and Bod, 2011; Fossum and Levy, 2012; van Schijndel and Schuler, 2015). The argument concerns the strength of the fitted coefficients for different types of grammatical predictors. These "language model" predictors contribute to varying degrees in regression models of the eye-fixation record. In certain cases, it appears that higher-order structure — for instance, phrase structure — is unhelpful. On the other hand, other cases suggest that higher-order structure does shine through in the eye-movement record. In this debate, fitted coefficients on the more linguistically-sophisticated predictors have been taken to quantify the veridicality of the Competence Hypothesis. The linguistic predictors that researchers examine qualify as "basic components" to the extent that they improve the regression model that they are part of.

Of course, psycholinguists have known for a long time that low-level factors such as word frequency and bigram probability are useful in explaining eye-fixation times (Thibadeau et al., 1982; McDonald and Shillcock, 2003). These are not relevant to the Competence Hypothesis. Rather, the action is with higher-order factors: predictors based on larger domains of locality, as defined by grammars that could plausibly play a role in the best descrip-

Proceedings of CMCL 2015, pages 89–97,
Denver, Colorado, June 4, 2015.

tion of language as a structural system.

The research reported in this paper adopts the same model-comparison methodology as Frank, Fossum, van Schijndel and their co-authors. But it applies this method to spatially localized neural time courses obtained using fMRI. Using grammatical predictors at six different levels of "richness" we compare a family of nested regression models. We find that phrase structure in the style of the Penn Treebank (Marcus et al., 1993) improves a regression, over and above various n-gram baselines. X-bar structures generated by Minimalist Grammars (Stabler, 1997, 2011) improve yet further over that. This holds for time courses taken from anterior temporal lobe (aTL), an area that has been implicated in "basic syntactic processing" (Friederici and Gierhan, 2013). But only the n-gram predictors are useful in modeling time courses from inferior frontal gyrus (IFG), a traditional syntax area (Grodzinsky and Friederici, 2006). Section 6 discusses this pattern of results in light of other work on naturalistic language comprehension.

2 Methods and Materials

The methodology follows Brennan et al. (2012) in the use of spoken narrative as a stimulus. Participants listen to an audiobook while in the scanner. The sequence of images collected during the spoken presentation becomes the dependent variable in a regression against a times series of linguistic predictors derived from the text of the story. In contrast to the work of Frank, Fossum and van Schijndel, we used auditory rather than visual presentation.

Participants

Thirteen college-age volunteers (6 women) participated for pay, but we excluded two individuals whose inferred head-movements exceeded 0.6mm or had eight or more movements $\geq$0.1mm. All qualified as right-handed on the Edinburgh handedness inventory (Oldfield, 1971). They self-identified as native English speakers and gave their informed consent.

Data Collection

Imaging was performed using a 3T MRI scanner (Discovery MR750, GE Healthcare, Milwaukee, WI) with a 32-channel head coil at the Cornell MRI Facility. Blood Oxygen Level Dependent (BOLD) signals were collected using a T2*-weighted echo planar imaging (EPI) sequence (repetition time: 2000 ms, echo time: 27 ms, flip angle: 77deg, image acceleration: 2X, field of view: 216 x 216 mm, matrix size 72 x 72, and 44 oblique slices, yielding 3 mm isotropic voxels). Anatomical images were collected with a high resolution T1-weighted (1 x 1 x 1 mm^3 voxel) with a Magnetization-Prepared RApid Gradient-Echo (MP-RAGE) pulse sequence.

Presentation

Auditory stimuli were delivered through MRI-safe, high-fidelity headphones (Confon HP-VS01, MR Confon, Magdeburg, Germany) inside the head coil. The headphones were secured against the plastic frame of the coil using foam blocks. Using a spoken recitation of the US Constitution, an experimenter increased the volume until participants reported that they could hear clearly.

Stimuli

The audio stimulus was Kristin McQuillan's reading of the first chapter of Lewis Carroll's Alice in Wonderland from `librivox.org`. We chose this text both because of its use in prior imaging work (Brennan et al., 2012) and because fine-grained syntactic annotations are available for it. We used Praat to normalize the spoken-language audio signal to 70dB and dilate it by 20%. This slowed speech improved comprehension in the scanner. The audio presentation lasted 12.4 minutes. Upon emerging from the scanner, participants completed a twelve-question, multiple-choice quiz concerning events and situations described in the story.

3 Data analysis

Preprocessing

We used SPM8 (Friston et al., 2007) to spatially-realign functional images (EPI) and co-register them with participants' structural images (MP-RAGE). Smoothing was 3mm isotropic, and SPM8's ICBM template was used to put the data into MNI stereotaxic coordinates.

Linking hypotheses

We linked linguistic structures (e.g. POS tag sequences, Penn-style trees, X-bar trees) to predictions about BOLD signal in two different ways.

Link #1: Surprisal

For probabilistic language models, we linked the probability of a word in its left-context to BOLD signal using the log-reciprocal of the probability of the next word. This is "surprisal" in the sense of Hale (2001).

Link #2: Node Count

With non-probabilistic grammars, we linked the syntactic structure of a sentence to the BOLD signal it evokes by counting the number of tree nodes between successive words, including "empty" nodes such as the traces of movement. This link expresses the basic claim that more grammatical structure implies greater comprehension effort. While intuitive, the precise formulation of this idea has been tricky; see Frazier (1985, section 4.4) for critical discussion. Our two node count hypotheses were based, respectively, on top-down and bottom-up parsing (see e.g. Hale, 2014, chapter 3). The top-down traversal that we used enumerates nodes in a depth-first, left to right order analogous to an LL parser. The bottom-up traversal that we used enumerates daughters before mothers in the manner of a shift-reduce LR parser. Taking the stimulus text to be largely unambiguous for native English-speaking listeners, we assume a perfect oracle that enumerates nodes of just the correct tree.

Hemodynamic Response

Via these linking hypotheses, we derived time series of predictions about the effortfulness of comprehending each word in the text. Following Just & Varma (2007) we convolved these time series with SPM8's canonical hemodynamic response function (HRF) to arrive at an expected BOLD signal. This HRF is a difference of Gamma functions (Friston et al., 2007, chapter 14). Figure 1 summarizes this methodology graphically.

Regions of interest

By defining an impulse at the offset of each spoken word, an atheoretical predictor call Rate local-

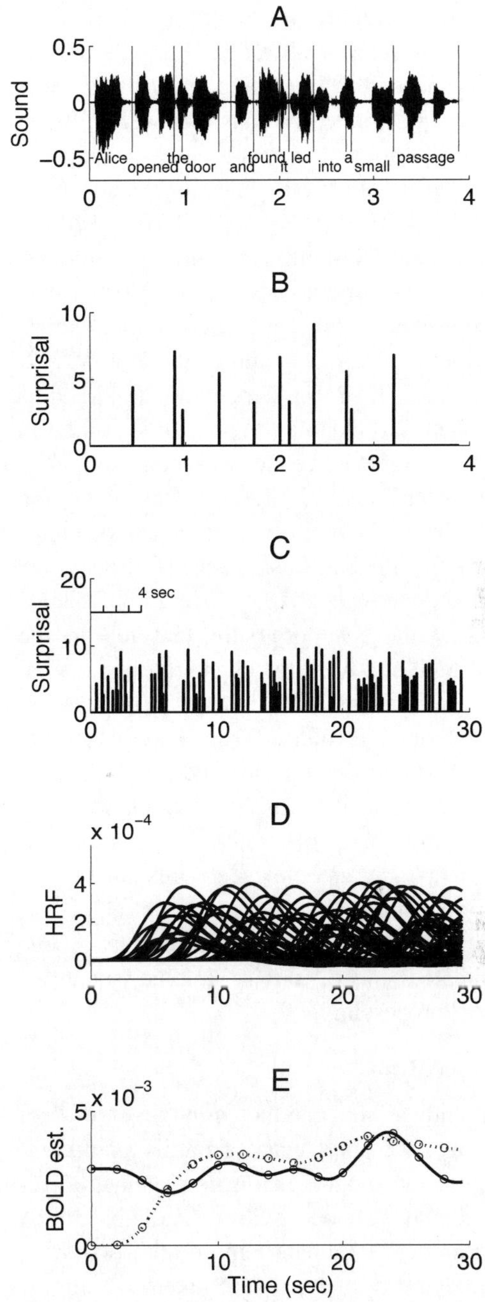

Figure 1: Deriving an expected BOLD signal from a sequence of linguistic structures (analogous to Fig. 11 of Just & Varma (2007)): (A) Segmentation of a spoken narrative (B) Complexity metric, such as surprisal, defines intensity of point event (C) Points shown over a longer interval (D) Points convolved with canonical HRF (E) Summed HRFs yield estimate of BOLD response (dotted) made orthogonal to low-level covariates (solid).

izes brain regions whose BOLD signal varies in time with the speech stimulus. We localized spherical regions of interest, each with radius 10mm, centered on the maxima of the Rate predictor within three anatomically-constrained regions that were defined based on prior work on the neural bases of syntax.

Maxima for this predictor that fell bilaterally in temporal lobe anterior to Heschl's Gyrus served to define the center of left and right anterior temporal region. Anterior temporal lobe has shown sensitivity to the presence vs. absence of constituent structure (Stowe et al., 1998; Vandenberghe et al., 2002; Humphries et al., 2006; Snijders et al., 2009; Bemis and Pylkkänen, 2011; Pallier et al., 2011) and brain damage to this region correlates with deficits in morphosyntax (Dronkers et al., 2004). These data, and others, have led to the proposal that the anterior temporal lobe is involved in "basic syntactic processes." (Friederici and Gierhan, 2013, p. 252).

Maxima of the Rate predictor that fell in the left frontal lobe and were listed as "inferior frontal gyrus" in the Harvard-Oxford Brain Atlas defined the center of our left inferior frontal gyrus region. Numerous findings from lesion-induced syntactic deficits (Caramazza and Zurif, 1976; Grodzinsky, 2000) and neuroimaging of brain activations for simple and syntactically complex sentences (Just et al., 1996; Stromswold et al., 1996; Stowe et al., 1998; Snijders et al., 2009; Santi and Grodzinsky, 2007) have implicated this region in various aspects of grammatical processing.

Statistical Analysis

Statistical analysis was conducted in two stages. In the first stage, we constructed a family of mixed-effects regression models using non-syntactic predictors together with one syntax predictor drawn from each model. Parameters more than two standard errors away from zero were taken to "significant" in this analysis (Gelman and Hill, 2007).

In the second stage we conducted a set of stepwise model comparisons to evaluate the unique contribution of each "grain size" which showed a significant contribution in stage one. Comparisons were evaluated using likelihood ratio tests. Models were nested in order of smallest to largest grain size (i.e. amount of hierarchy), and least to most predictive for measures of node count. The list of fixed effects for each model entered in to this comparison is given in Table 1.

All models included fixed effects for word Rate (see above), log unigram frequency, and three principle components representing head-movements, heart rate, and lung action. A fixed effect for prosodic breaks was also included to control for correlations between acoustic variance and syntactic structure. This predictor is a perceptual judgment of break index strength made in light of ToBI annotation guidelines by two independent raters. Subjects were treated as a random intercept in all models.

4 Structure at various grain sizes

Markov Models

2gram.l, 2gram.p, 3gram.l, 3gram.p – We used OpenGRM to fit Markov Models of various orders (Allauzen et al., 2007). These models were trained on the version of Alice in Wonderland that is distributed by Project Gutenberg, etext # 11. As a preprocessing step, chapter headings were removed and all words converted to lowercase. Lexicalized (*.l*) and unlexicalized POS (*.p*) models were created.

Penn-style Phrase Structure

cfg.surp, cfg.bu, cfg.td – We used the EarleyX implementation of Stolcke's probabilistic Earley parser to compute surprisal values from phrase structure grammars (Luong et al., 2013; Stolcke, 1995). We used a grammar whose rules came from Stanford parser output, when applied to the entire Alice in Wonderland book (Klein and Manning, 2003). Punctuation was removed. This renders the training data comparable across *cfg.surp* and $\{2,3\}$*gram*. The node count predictors were based on the same Penn-style structures as in Brennan et al. (2012).

X-bar Trees

mg.bu, mg.td – We used Minimalist Grammars to define more detailed analyses for each sentence. These grammars extend and reorganize the analyses discussed in Hale (2003, chapter 4) in a way that is guided by Sportiche, Koopman & Stabler (2013). They derive "X-bar" structural descriptions that integrate constituency, dependency and movement information. Figure 3 highlights a case where the X-bar predictor includes additional de-

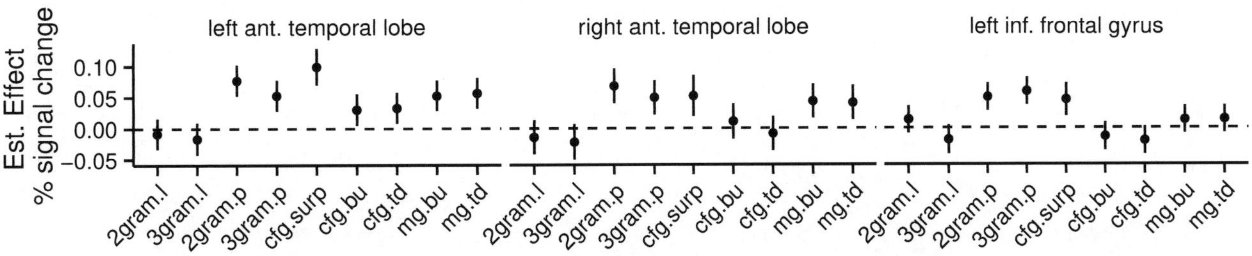

Figure 2: Magnitude of fitted coefficients across all syntax predictors, considered individually. Fine-grained linguistic structure from Penn-style *cfg.surp* and X-bar structures $mg.\{bu, td\}$ are positive predictors of the neural time-course in anterior temporal lobe. See Table 2 for stepwise model comparison.

tail, namely about movement. Of course, these trees encode many other aspects of sentence structure that are treated in Minimalist theories of syntax (see e.g. Adger (2003) or Hornstein, Nunes and Grohmann (2005) for an introduction). Traversing these trees in either Bottom-Up or Top-Down order, we obtain node counts analogous to those used in Brennan et al (2012).

model	*description*
Ø	lexical, prosodic, and physiological but no syntactic predictors
A	add POS tag 2-gram
B	add POS tag 3-gram
C	add CFG surprisal
D	add bottom-up CFG node count
E	add bottom-up X-bar node count
F	add top-down X-bar node count

Table 1: Nested models

5 Results

Fine-grained predictors based on X-bar trees and Penn-style phrase structure each improved a mixed-effects model of the neural time course in anterior temporal lobe during naturalistic story comprehension. This did not obtain in the time courses from inferior frontal gyrus. Figure 2 shows the estimated coefficients (± 2 standard errors) for each of the syntax predictors when included alone in a model with only word-level and physiological "nuisance" predictors. Table 2 reports a model comparison that tests which predictors contribute independently of other, coarser-grained predictors. It lists the steps that reached statistical significance at the $p < 0.05$ level for each ROI. Table 2 uses the letters A–F to identify increasingly refined models along a progression that is described in Table 1.

Performance on the post-scan was substantially higher (median=11) than chance (3 out of 12). This confirms that participants were indeed attending to the story.

left aTL	*predictor*	$\chi^2(1)$	*p*
Ø to A	2gram.p	38.9	$< .001$
B to C	cfg.surp	22.3	$< .001$
D to E	mg.bu	5.5	< 0.05
right aTL			
Ø to A	2gram.p	23.7	$< .001$
D to E	mg.bu	4.3	< 0.05
left IFG			
Ø to A	2gram.p	19.6	$< .001$
A to B	3gram.p	8.4	$< .01$

Table 2: Statistically-significant steps in a model comparison

6 Discussion

As Figure 2 indicates, a variety of grammatical predictors turned out to be helpful in explaining BOLD signals. Even the most abstruse predictors that we considered, ones based on X-bar structures generated by Minimalist Grammars, led to reliable improvements over baseline models. This suggests

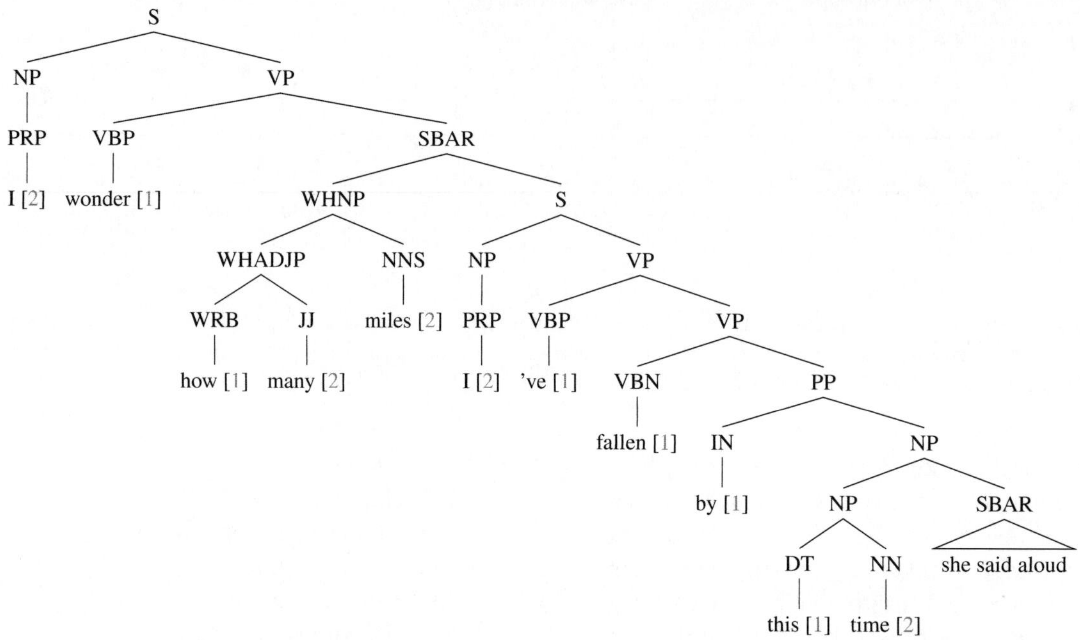

(a) Coarse-grained Penn-style structure. Bracketted numbers show the value of *cfg.bu* at each word.

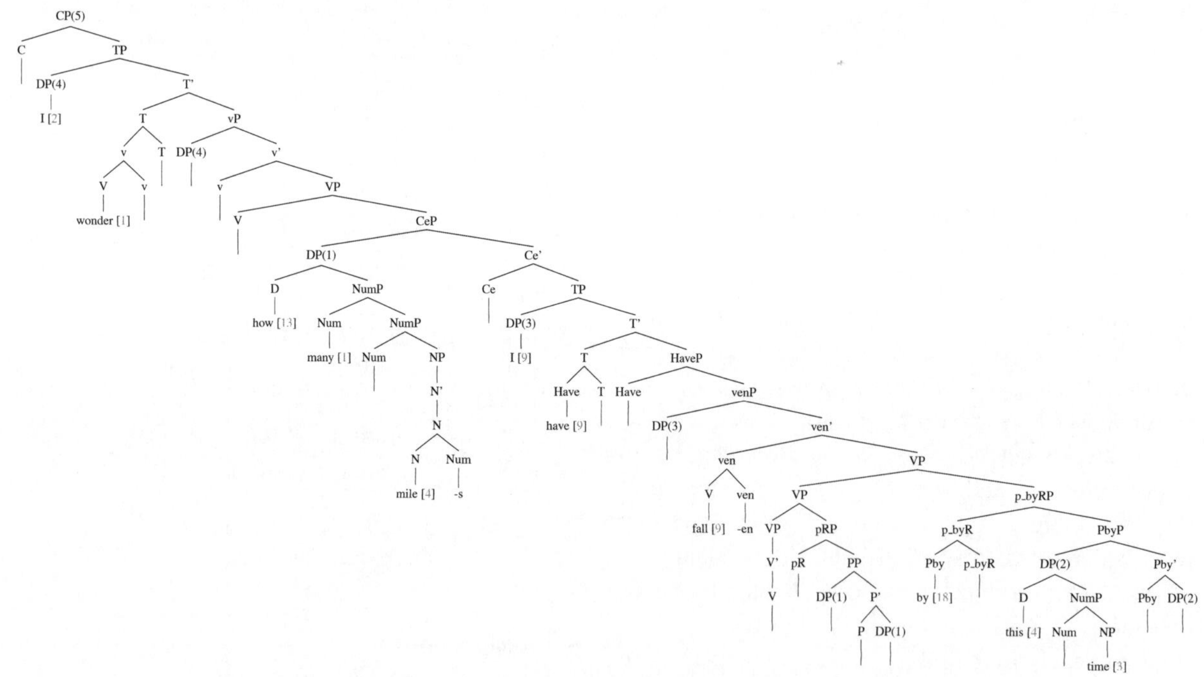

(b) Fine-grained X-bar structure. Bracketted numbers show the value of *mg.bu* at each word.

Figure 3: Coarse-grained versus fine-grained syntactic analyses of the same sentence. Numbers in square brackets are BOLD signal predictors. They reflect the presence of empty nodes in 3(b) but not 3(a). This aspect of the structure impacts the prediction at the word "by".

that indeed, the human sentence processing system is sensitive to hierarchical structure at least in the anterior temporal lobe. It is possible that the null result reported by Frank et al. (2011; 2015) reflects the difficulty of measuring nuanced syntactic processing activity with behavioral and ERP measures.

While n-gram predictors were helpful throughout, Penn phrase structures and X-bar structures did not gain purchase in inferior frontal gyrus the way they did in anterior temporal regions. This "aTL-specificity" corroborates earlier findings that used node count but not surprisal (Brennan et al., 2012).

The bilateral character of the aTL results aligns well with related work with written stimuli by Wehbe et al (2014). Using word features related to labelled dependency arcs (i.e. noun modifier, verbal complement) and part of speech tags, Wehbe and colleagues found a cluster of voxels in right anterior temporal lobe where syntactic information contributed to high performance in a classification-by-prediction task. This points to a temporal lobe language network whose normal mode of operation employs both hemispheres.

7 Conclusion

If we take the model comparison approach — as applied to neural time courses — to be an empirical test of the Competence Hypothesis, then the Hypothesis survives. These data support the view that humans use linguistic structure to comprehend spoken narratives. This finding re-prompts the question that occupied Bresnan, Kaplan, Steedman & Stabler: which linguistic theory is most helpful in understanding that comprehension? Answering this question is more than one lab can manage. We therefore plan to release this time course data so that the broader cognitive science community can try out alternative models based on a wider variety of parsing theories.

Acknowledgments

With sadness we acknowledge our deceased collaborator, Sarah Van Wagenen, who passed away before this work was finished. We are grateful to Edward P. Stabler, Jr. for conceptual and practical help with this project, and to Rob Mason for valuable discussions. We also thank the students of LING7710: Frederick Callaway, Elana Feldman, Jaclyn Jeffrey-Wilensky and Adam Mahar. This project was supported in part by NIH grant 1S10RR025145 and NSF CAREER award number 0741666.

References

David Adger. 2003. *Core Syntax: a Minimalist Approach*. Oxford University Press.

Cyril Allauzen, Michael Riley, Johan Schalkwyk, Wojciech Skut, and Mehryar Mohri. 2007. OpenFst: A general and efficient weighted finite-state transducer library. In *Proceedings of the* 12th *International Conference on Implementation and Application of Automata*, pages 11–23. Springer.

Douglas K. Bemis and Liina Pylkkänen. 2011. Simple composition: A magnetoencephalography investigation into the comprehension of minimal linguistic phrases. *The Journal of Neuroscience*, 31(8):2801–2814.

Jonathan Brennan, Yuval Nir, Uri Hasson, Rafael Malach, David J. Heeger, and Liina Pylkkäen. 2012. Syntactic structure building in the anterior temporal lobe during natural story listening. *Brain and Language*, 120(2):163 – 173.

Joan Bresnan and Ronald M. Kaplan. 1982. Introduction: Grammars as mental representations of language. In Joan Bresnan, editor, *The Mental Representation of Grammatical Relations*, pages xvii,lii. MIT Press, Cambridge, MA.

Alfonso Caramazza and Edgard B. Zurif. 1976. Dissociation of algorithmic and heuristic processes in language comprehension: Evidence from aphasia. *Brain and Language*, 3(4):572–582.

Noam Chomsky. 1965. *Aspects of the Theory of Syntax*. MIT Press.

Nina F. Dronkers, David P. Wilkins, Robert D. Van Valin, Brenda B. Redfern, and Jeri J. Jaeger. 2004. Lesion analysis of the brain areas involved in language comprehension: Towards a new functional anatomy of language. *Cognition*, 92(1-2):145–177.

Victoria Fossum and Roger Levy. 2012. Sequential vs. hierarchical syntactic models of human incremental sentence processing. In *Proceedings of the 3rd Annual Workshop on Cognitive Modeling and Computational Linguistics*, pages 61–69, Montreal, Quebec.

Stefan L. Frank and Rens Bod. 2011. Insensitivity of the human sentence-processing system to hierarchical structure. *Psychological Science*, 22(6):829–34, June.

Stefan L. Frank, Leun J. Otten, Giulia Galli, and Gabriella Vigliocco. 2015. The ERP response to the amount of information conveyed by words in sentences. *Brain and Language*, 140(0):1–11.

Lyn Frazier. 1985. Syntactic complexity. In David R. Dowty, Lauri Karttunen, and Arnold M. Zwicky, editors, *Natural language parsing: Psychological, computational, and theoretical perspectives*, chapter 4, pages 129–189. Cambridge University Press.

Angela D. Friederici and Sarah M.E. Gierhan. 2013. The language network. *Current Opinion in Neurobiology*, 23(2):250 – 254.

Karl J. Friston, John Ashburner, Stefan J. Kiebel, Thomas E. Nichols, and Wiliam D. Penny, editors. 2007. *Statistical Parametric Mapping: The Analysis of Functional Brain Images*. Academic Press.

Andrew Gelman and Jennifer Hill. 2007. *Data Analysis Using Regression and Multilevel/Hierarchical Models*. Cambridge University Press.

Yosef Grodzinsky and Angela D. Friederici. 2006. Neuroimaging of syntax and syntactic processing. *Current Opinion in Neurobiology*, 16(2):240–246.

Yosef Grodzinsky. 2000. The neurology of syntax: Language use without Broca's area. *Behavioral and Brain Sciences*, 23(01):1–21.

John Hale. 2001. A probabilistic Earley parser as a psycholinguistic model. In *Proceedings of the Second Meeting of the North American Chapter of the Association for Computational Linguistics*.

John Hale. 2003. *Grammar, uncertainty and sentence processing*. Ph.D. thesis, Johns Hopkins University, Baltimore, Maryland.

John Hale. 2014. Automaton theories of human sentence comprehension. CSLI Publications, September.

Norbert Hornstein, Jairo Nunes, and Kleanthes K. Grohmann. 2005. *Understanding Minimalism*. Cambridge University Press.

Colin Humphries, Jeffrey R. Binder, David A. Medler, and Einat Liebenthal. 2006. Syntactic and semantic modulation of neural activity during auditory sentence comprehension. *Journal of Cognitive Neuroscience*, 18(4):665–679.

Marcel Just and Sashank Varma. 2007. The organization of thinking: What functional brain imaging reveals about the neuroarchitecture of complex cognition. *Cognitive, Affective, & Behavioral Neuroscience*, 7:153–191.

Marcel A. Just, Patricia A. Carpenter, Timothy A. Keller, William F. Eddy, and Keith R. Thulborn. 1996. Brain activation modulated by sentence comprehension. *Science*, 274(5284):114–116.

Dan Klein and Christopher D. Manning. 2003. Accurate unlexicalized parsing. In *Proceedings of the 41st Annual Meeting of the Association for Computational Linguistics*, pages 423–430, Sapporo, Japan, July. Association for Computational Linguistics.

Minh-Thang Luong, Michael C. Frank, and Mark Johnson. 2013. Parsing entire discourses as very long strings: Capturing topic continuity in grounded language learning. *Transactions of the Association for Computational Linguistics*, 1(3):315–323.

Mitchell P. Marcus, Beatrice Santorini, and Mary Ann Marcinkiewicz. 1993. Building a large annotated corpus of English: the Penn Treebank. *Computational Linguistics*, 19:313–330.

Scott A. McDonald and Richard C. Shillcock. 2003. Low-level predictive inference in reading: the influence of transitional probabilities on eye movements. *Vision Research*, 43(16):1735–1751.

Richard C. Oldfield. 1971. The assessment and analysis of handedness: the Edinburgh inventory. *Neuropsychologia*, 9(1):97–113.

Christophe Pallier, Anne-Dominique Devauchelle, and Stanislas Dehaene. 2011. Cortical representation of the constituent structure of sentences. *Proceedings of the National Academy of Sciences*, 108(6):2522–2527, 02.

Andrea Santi and Yosef Grodzinsky. 2007. Working memory and syntax interact in Broca's area. *NeuroImage*, 37(1):8–17.

Tineke M. Snijders, Theo Vosse, Gerard Kempen, Jos J.A. Van Berkum, Karl Magnus Petersson, and Peter Hagoort. 2009. Retrieval and unification of syntactic structure in sentence comprehension: an fmri study using word-category ambiguity. *Cerebral Cortex*, 19(7):1493–1503.

Dominique Sportiche, Hilda Koopman, and Edward Stabler. 2013. *An Introduction to Syntactic Analysis and Theory*. Wiley-Blackwell.

Edward Stabler. 1991. Avoid the pedestrian's paradox. In Robert C. Berwick, Steven P. Abney, and Carol Tenny, editors, *Principle-Based Parsing: computation and psycholinguistics*, Studies in Linguistics and Philosophy, pages 199–237. Kluwer, Dordrecht.

Edward Stabler. 1997. Derivational minimalism. In Christian Retoré, editor, *Logical Aspects of Computational Linguistics*, pages 68–95. Springer.

Edward P. Stabler. 2011. Computational perspectives on minimalism. In *The Oxford Handbook of Linguistic Minimalism*, chapter 27. Oxford University Press.

Mark Steedman. 1989. Grammar, interpretation and processing from the lexicon. In William Marslen-Wilson, editor, *Lexical Representation and Process*, chapter 16, pages 463–504. MIT Press, Cambridge, MA.

Andreas Stolcke. 1995. An efficient probabilistic context-free parsing algorithm that computes prefix probabilities. *Computational Linguistics*, 21(2):165–201.

Laurie A. Stowe, Cees A. J. Broere, Anne M. J. Paans, Albertus A. Wijers, Gijsbertus Mulder, Wim Vaalburg, and Frans Zwarts. 1998. Localizing components of a complex task: Sentence processing and working memory. *Neuroreport*, 9(13):2995–2999.

Karin Stromswold, David Caplan, Nathaniel Alpert, and Scott Rauch. 1996. Localization of syntactic comprehension by positron emission tomography. *Brain and Language*, 52:452–473.

Robert Thibadeau, Marcel A. Just, and Patricia Carpenter. 1982. A model of the time course and content of reading. *Cognitive Science*, 6:157–203.

Marten van Schijndel and William Schuler. 2015. Hierarchic syntax improves reading time prediction. In *Proceedings of NAACL 2015*, Denver, Colorado, USA, June. Association for Computational Linguistics.

Rik R.C. Vandenberghe, Anna C. Nobre, and Cathy J. Price. 2002. The response of left temporal cortex to sentences. *Journal of Cognitive Neuroscience*, 14(4):550–560, 05.

Leila Wehbe, Brian Murphy, Partha Talukdar, Alona Fyshe, Aaditya Ramdas, and Tom Mitchell. 2014. Simultaneously uncovering the patterns of brain regions involved in different story reading subprocesses. *PLOS ONE*, 9(11):e112575, November.

Author Index

Association for Computational Linguistics
209 N. Eighth Street
Stroudsburg, Pennsylvania 18360

CURRAN ASSOCIATES INC
proceedings
.com